# Wok Vegetarian Asian Cookbook

2 Books In 1: 150 Recipes For Stir Fry Dishes And Veggie Food From Asia

By

**Yoko Rice**
**Maki Blanc**

# VEGETARIAN ASIAN
## COOKBOOK

Typical Veggie Dishes from Thai Chinese Japanese and Indian Cuisines in 80 Recipes.

By

**Yoko Rice**

© **Copyright 2021 by Yoko Rice - All rights reserved.**

This document is geared towards providing exact and reliable information in regard to the topic and issue covered. The publication is sold with the idea that the publisher is not required to render accounting, officially permitted, or otherwise, qualified services. If advice is necessary, legal or professional, a practiced individual in the profession should be ordered.

From a Declaration of Principles which was accepted and approved equally by a Committee of the American Bar Association and a Committee of Publishers and Associations.

In no way is it legal to reproduce, duplicate, or transmit any part of this document in either electronic means or in printed format. Recording of this publication is strictly prohibited and any storage of this document is not allowed unless with written permission from the publisher. All rights reserved.

The information provided herein is stated to be truthful and consistent, in that any liability, in terms of inattention or otherwise, by any usage or abuse of any policies, processes, or directions contained within is the solitary and utter responsibility of the recipient reader. Under no circumstances will any legal responsibility or blame be held against the publisher for any reparation, damages, or monetary loss due to the information herein, either directly or indirectly.

Respective authors own all copyrights not held by the publisher.

The information herein is offered for informational purposes solely and is universal as so. The presentation of the information is without contract or any type of guarantee assurance.

The trademarks that are used are without any consent, and the publication of the trademark is without permission or backing by the trademark owner. All trademarks and brands within this book are for clarifying purposes only and are owned by the owners themselves, not affiliated with this document.

# Contents

INTRODUCTION ..................................................................... 10

CHAPTER 1: VEGETARIAN THAI RECIPES ................. 12

1.1 Banana and White Bean Yellow Curry Recipe .................... 12

1.2 Chargrilled Aubergine with Thai Basil Tofu Recipe ........... 14

1.3 Slow Cooker Pumpkin and Cauliflower Curry Recipe ........ 16

1.4 Vegetable Chips with Peanut Dip Recipe .......................... 18

1.5 Coriander and Cucumber Salad Recipe ............................. 19

1.6 Mushroom and Coconut Curry Recipe .............................. 20

1.7 Tofu in Green Coconut Curry Recipe ................................ 22

1.8 Butternut Squash and Red Curry Soup Recipe ................. 24

1.9 Oyster Mushrooms in Rice Noodles Recipe ...................... 26

1.10 Ginger and Coconut Rice Recipe .................................... 28

1.11 Warm Egg and Potato Salad with Spicy Peanut Sauce Recipe ............................................................................... 30

1.12 Thai Quorn with Rive Recipe ......................................... 32

1.13 Mango and Tofu Patties Recipe ...................................... 34

1.14 Creamy Roast Pepper Soup Recipe ................................ 36

1.15 Coconut and Pea Curry Recipe ...................................... 38

1.16 Mix Mushroom and Vegetable Salad Recipe ................... 40

1.17 Thai Lemongrass and Tofu Curry Recipe ....................... 42

1.18 Thai Peanut and Mango Salad Recipe .................. 44

1.19 Spicy Thai Green Papaya Soup Recipe ................ 46

1.20 Spicy Thai Bean Fritters Recipe .......................... 48

## CHAPTER 2: VEGETARIAN CHINESE RECIPES ........ 49

2.1 Chinese Green Bean Chow Mein Recipe ............... 49

2.2 Chinese General Tso Tofu Recipe ........................ 51

2.3 Chinese Fried Okra Salad Recipe ........................ 53

2.4 Spiced Cashew Vegetables Recipe ....................... 55

2.5 Spiced Mushroom Dumplings Recipe ................... 57

2.6 Vegetarian Tofu Wonton Recipe .......................... 59

2.7 Honey Chili Potatoes Recipe ............................... 61

2.8 Shitake Fried Rice Recipe ................................... 63

2.9 Vegetable Manchow Soup Recipe ........................ 65

2.10 Vegetable Chopsuey Recipe ............................... 67

2.11 Vegetarian Hakka Noodles Recipe ..................... 69

2.12 Chili Paneer Dry Recipe .................................... 71

2.13 Crunchy Iceberg Dumplings Recipe ................... 73

2.14 Chestnut Fried Rice Recipe ............................... 75

2.15 Chili and Garlic Noodles Recipe ........................ 77

2.16 Ricotta Wontons Recipe .................................... 79

2.17 Spiced Tofu Hotpot Recipe ................................ 81

2.18 Oyster and Spinach Stir-Fry Recipe .................. 83

2.19 Spiced Chickpea Stir-Fry Recipe ................................. 85

2.20 Carrot Dumplings Recipe ............................................. 87

## CHAPTER 3: VEGETARIAN JAPANESE RECIPES ....... 89

3.1 Creamy Asparagus Pasta Recipe .................................. 89

3.2 Teriyaki Sauce Vegetables Recipe ................................ 91

3.3 Vegetarian Soufflé Pancakes Recipe ............................. 92

3.4 Japanese Miso Rice Recipe .......................................... 94

3.5 Kabocha Soup Recipe .................................................. 96

3.6 Miso Vegetable Curry Recipe ....................................... 98

3.7 Teriyaki Tofu Dry Recipe ............................................ 100

3.8 Inari Tofu Recipe ........................................................ 102

3.9 Spicy Soba Soup Recipe ............................................. 104

3.10 Mashed Green Beans and Tofu Salad Recipe .............. 106

3.11 Spicy Eggplant Donburi Recipe ................................. 108

3.12 Udon Soup Recipe .................................................... 110

3.13 Spicy Tofu Katsu Recipe ........................................... 112

3.14 Vegetable Teppanyaki Recipe .................................... 114

3.15 Vegetarian Okonomiyaki Recipe ................................ 116

3.16 Vegetarian Sukiyaki Recipe ....................................... 118

3.17 Spicy Corn Soup Recipe ............................................ 120

3.18 Teriyaki Mushroom Skewers Recipe .......................... 122

3.19 Vegetarian Gyoza Recipe .......................................... 123

3.20 Japanese Kale Soup Recipe............................................125

## CHAPTER 4: VEGETARIAN INDIAN RECIPES ..........127

4.1 Roasted Zucchini in Curry Oatmeal Recipe....................127

4.2 Spicy Banana Curry Recipe................................................129

4.3 Spiced Tofu Skewers Recipe................................................131

4.4 Indian Mushroom Rice Recipe .........................................132

4.5 Spicy Palak Tofu Paneer Recipe .......................................134

4.6 Vegetarian Korma Recipe.................................................136

4.7 Indian Cauliflower and Pea Curry Recipe .....................138

4.8 Spicy Chickpea and Mushroom Curry Recipe .................140

4.9 Spicy Pav Bhaji Recipe ......................................................142

4.10 Indian Roasted Brussel Sprouts Recipe ........................144

4.11 Indian Sultani Daal Recipe..............................................145

4.12 Indian Curried Okra and Eggplant with Chickpea Recipe ..................................................................................................147

4.13 Creamy Halloumi Recipe..................................................149

4.14 Indian Bottle Gourd Dal Recipe......................................151

4.15 Indian Cabbage Palya Recipe..........................................153

4.16 Spicy Kale and Potato Curry Recipe..............................155

4.17 Indian Mint Rice Recipe ..................................................157

4.18 Indian Garlic Butter Naan Bread Recipe ......................159

4.19 Indian Mango Curry Recipe............................................160

4.20 Indian Chickpea Pancakes Recipe .................................162

CONCLUSION ........................................................ **163**

# Introduction

All throughout the planet, individuals are eating more veggie food than ever. A few anthropologists accept that early people, for the most part, accumulated and ate plants. They enhanced a basically plant-based eating routine. Studies on the Stone Age or Paleolithic diet uncover that early people gathered up to 55 distinct sorts of plants to eat and depended intensely on vegan food varieties for nourishment and endurance.

Vegetarianism in Western societies is a genuinely new marvel, however not without antiquated points of reference. In numerous Asian societies, vegetarianism has been set up for quite a long time. The culinary and social parts of vegetarianism might be viewed as more profoundly created in some Asian societies.

Fish assumes an enormous part in numerous public foods, especially Japanese, Korean, Vietnamese and Thai. Meat utilization is firmly connected with big league salaries. Consequently, as Asian nations have modernized, meat utilization has risen. Despite the fact that suppositions vary between various schools and customs, the promotion of vegetarianism is firmly connected with Buddhism and different religions. Subsequently, veggie cafés in numerous Asian urban areas can regularly be found in nearness to sanctuaries.

There is a wide range of assortments of vegetables eaten in Asia. Chinese cabbage is high in nutrient C, which makes it a solid alternative for you. It is a magnificent expansion to servings of mixed greens, soups, or pan-fried food as well.

You will see the pattern with Asian vegetables is they all are high in supplements. The daikon radish is no exemption. It is high in supplements while staying low in calories. Bok choy is a vegetable high in many nutrients. It is likewise high in iron, calcium, potassium, magnesium and manganese. Taro root is another Asian vegetable high in various kinds of nutrients. Taro root likewise assists with managing your glucose levels, which is useful for those battling diabetes. Spinach assists with lessening your cholesterol, supports assimilation, assists with diabetes and is extraordinary for your heart wellbeing as well. There are various other vegetables that are eaten in Asia and are of high importance, such as peas, butternut squash, mushrooms, eggplants, and much more.

You will learn various different recipes originated from Asia in this book. This book contains 80 vegetarian recipes that are traditionally cooked in Asia. The recipe section will include Thai, Chinese, Japanese and Indian recipes. You do not have to order from an eatery any further to eat the best Asian food in town. You are all ready to cook with this cookbook by your side. So, start reading this amazing book now!

# Chapter 1: Vegetarian Thai Recipes

Thai vegetarian cuisine is a new world that you will love to explore. Thai recipes are used as comfort food by numerous individuals all around the world.

## 1.1 Banana and White Bean Yellow Curry Recipe

**Preparation Time:** 30 minutes
**Cooking Time:** 30 minutes
**Serving:** 4

### Ingredients:

- Two teaspoons of rice wine
- One teaspoon of caster sugar
- A quarter teaspoon of Sichuan pepper
- Two teaspoons of chopped red chili
- Half cup of spicy yellow paste
- Half teaspoon of turmeric powder
- Black pepper to taste
- Salt to taste
- One tablespoon of chopped ginger
- One tablespoon of chopped garlic
- Half cup of finely chopped spring onions

- Two tablespoons of sesame oil
- Four teaspoons of dark soy sauce
- Two cups of parboiled white beans
- Two cups of raw banana
- One cup of coconut milk

**Instructions:**
1. Take a large pan.
2. Heat the oil in a pan and add the spring onions in it.
3. Cook it until they become soft and golden brown in color.
4. Add the chopped ginger and garlic into the pan.
5. Add the beans and stir fry until the color changes.
6. Add the rice wine and raw banana in the pan.
7. Cook the mixture well for about ten minutes until they are roasted.
8. Add coconut milk, caster sugar, spicy yellow paste, white pepper, turmeric powder, red chili pepper, dark soy sauce, black pepper, and salt into the pan.
9. Add the rest of the ingredients into the mixture.
10. Cook the ingredients well for about fifteen to twenty minutes.
11. Your dish is ready to be served.

## 1.2 Chargrilled Aubergine with Thai Basil Tofu Recipe

**Preparation Time:** 30 minutes
**Cooking Time:** 20 minutes
**Serving:** 4

**Ingredients:**

- One tablespoon of hoisin sauce
- One tablespoon of sriracha sauce
- Half cup of chopped celery
- Half cup of sliced green onions
- One teaspoon of rice wine
- One teaspoon of fresh ginger
- One tablespoon of fish sauce
- One tablespoon of soy sauce
- One teaspoon of Thai five spice
- Two tablespoons of chili garlic sauce
- Half cup of bamboo shoots
- Half cup of fresh cilantro leaves
- A quarter cup of fresh basil leaves
- One cup of vegetable broth
- Two cups of grilled eggplant
- Two cups of tofu cubes
- One teaspoon of chopped garlic

- Two tablespoons of vegetable oil

**Instructions:**
1. Take a wok.
2. Add the hoisin sauce, sriracha sauce, chopped garlic, Thai spice, chili garlic sauce, basil leaves, and ginger into the wok.
3. Add the vegetable broth and sauces into the wok mixture.
4. Cook the dish for ten minutes.
5. Add the tofu pieces into the mixture.
6. Mix the tofu well and cook it for five minutes.
7. Cook the ingredients well and mix them with the rest of the ingredients.
8. Reduce the heat of the stove.
9. Add the eggplant pieces, chopped basil leaves, and the rest of the ingredients into the pan.
10. Cook the dish for fifteen more minutes.
11. Add the cilantro to the dish.
12. Your dish is ready to be served.

## 1.3 Slow Cooker Pumpkin and Cauliflower Curry Recipe

**Preparation Time:** 10 minutes
**Cooking Time:** 60 minutes
**Serving:** 2

**Ingredients:**

- One pound cauliflower and pumpkin
- Two tablespoon Thai curry paste
- One cup diced basil leaves
- Two tablespoon coconut cream
- Two tablespoon olive oil
- Half cup vegetable stock
- One cup of chopped
- One tablespoon soy sauce
- Salt to taste
- Black pepper to taste
- Chopped fresh cilantro leaves
- One cup of coconut milk

**Instructions:**
1. Take a pan.

2. Add the oil and onions in it.
3. Cook the onions until they become soft and fragrant.
4. Add the chopped garlic into it.
5. Add the cauliflower and pumpkin pieces and cook them until they start to change color.
6. Cook the mixture and add the tomatoes into it.
7. Add the bay leaves, Thai curry paste, freshly chopped basil leaves, and some water in it.
8. Mix the ingredients carefully and cover the pan.
9. Add the coconut cream into the mixture.
10. Add the coconut milk and soy sauce into the mixture.
11. Add the water into the mixture and cover the pan.
12. Let the curry cook for ten to fifteen minutes straight.
13. Add the chopped cilantro on top.
14. Your dish is ready to be served.

# 1.4 Vegetable Chips with Peanut Dip Recipe

**Preparation Time:** 30 minutes
**Cooking Time:** 10 minutes
**Serving:** 4

**Ingredients:**

- Two cups of peanut dip
- Two tablespoons of minced garlic
- Two tablespoons of minced ginger
- Half cup of cilantro
- One cup of oil
- Two tablespoons of cornflour
- One teaspoon of Thai spice powder
- Two cups of mixed vegetables

**Instructions:**
1. Take a bowl.
2. Add all the ingredients except oil and peanut dip into the bowl.
3. Mix everything well.
4. Take a pan and heat it well.
5. Pour the oil in the pan.

6. Fry the vegetables in the pan.
7. Dish out when they turn crispy.
8. Your dish is ready to be served with peanut dip.

## 1.5 Coriander and Cucumber Salad Recipe

**Preparation Time:** 15 minutes
**Cooking Time:** 5 minutes
**Serving:** 4

**Ingredients:**

- Two tablespoons of sesame seeds
- One tablespoon of rice vinegar
- One teaspoon of sesame oil
- Two tablespoons of white sugar
- Salt to taste
- Black pepper to taste
- A quarter cup of olive oil
- Two cups of cucumber pieces
- One cup of chopped coriander

**Instructions:**
1. Take a skillet and add the sesame seeds into it.

2. Toast the seeds until they turn golden brown and fragrant.
3. Take a bowl and add the sesame oil, vinegar, olive oil, and sugar into it.
4. Add the coriander and cucumber into the bowl.
5. Mix all the ingredients well.
6. Top it with toasted sesame seeds.
7. Your dish is ready to be served.

## 1.6 Mushroom and Coconut Curry Recipe

**Preparation Time:** 30 minutes
**Cooking Time:** 30 minutes
**Serving:** 4

**Ingredients:**

- Two teaspoons of rice wine
- One teaspoon of caster sugar
- A quarter teaspoon of Sichuan pepper
- Two teaspoons of chopped red chili
- Half teaspoon of turmeric powder
- Black pepper to taste
- Salt to taste
- One tablespoon of chopped ginger
- One tablespoon of chopped garlic

- Half cup of finely chopped spring onions
- Two tablespoons of sesame oil
- Four teaspoons of dark soy sauce
- Two cups of mushrooms
- One cup of coconut milk

**Instructions:**
1. Take a large pan.
2. Heat the oil in a pan and add the spring onions in it.
3. Cook it until they become soft and golden brown in color.
4. Add the chopped ginger and garlic into the pan.
5. Add the mushrooms, rice wine and stir fry it until the color changes.
6. Cook the mixture well for about ten minutes until they are roasted.
7. Add coconut milk, caster sugar, white pepper, turmeric powder, red chili pepper, dark soy sauce, black pepper, and salt into the pan.
8. Add the rest of the ingredients into the mixture.
9. Cook the ingredients well for about fifteen to twenty minutes.
10. Your dish is ready to be served.

## 1.7 Tofu in Green Coconut Curry Recipe

**Preparation Time:** 30 minutes
**Cooking Time:** 30 minutes
**Serving:** 4

**Ingredients:**

- Two teaspoons of rice wine
- One teaspoon of caster sugar
- A quarter teaspoon of Sichuan pepper
- Two teaspoons of chopped red chili
- Half cup of green curry paste
- Half teaspoon of turmeric powder
- Black pepper to taste
- Salt to taste
- One tablespoon of chopped ginger
- One tablespoon of chopped garlic
- Half cup of finely chopped spring onions
- Two tablespoons of sesame oil
- Four teaspoons of dark soy sauce
- Two cups of parboiled white beans
- One cup of coconut milk

**Instructions:**
1. Take a large pan.
2. Heat the oil in a pan and add the spring onions in it.
3. Cook it until they become soft and golden brown in color.
4. Add the chopped ginger and garlic into the pan.
5. Add the tofu and stir fry it until the color changes.
6. Add the rice wine and green curry paste in the pan.
7. Cook the mixture well for about ten minutes until they are roasted.
8. Add coconut milk, caster sugar, white pepper, turmeric powder, red chili pepper, dark soy sauce, black pepper, and salt into the pan.
9. Add the rest of the ingredients into the mixture.
10. Cook the ingredients well for about fifteen to twenty minutes.
11. Your dish is ready to be served.

# 1.8 Butternut Squash and Red Curry Soup Recipe

**Preparation Time:** 10 minutes
**Cooking Time:** 30 minutes
**Serving:** 2

**Ingredients:**

- One pound butternut squash
- Two tablespoons of red curry paste
- Two tablespoons of olive oil
- Half cup of vegetable stock
- One cup of chopped tomatoes
- One cup of onion
- Three cups of water
- One tablespoon of soy sauce
- Salt to taste
- Black pepper to taste
- Chopped fresh cilantro leaves
- One cup of coconut milk
- Fresh parsley
- Toasted sesame seeds

**Instructions:**
1. Take a pan.
2. Add the oil and onions in it.
3. Cook the onions until they become soft and fragrant.
4. Add the chopped garlic into it.
5. Add the butternut squash pieces into the mixture.
6. Cook the mixture and add the tomatoes into it.
7. Add the bay leaves, red curry paste, and some water in it.
8. Mix the ingredients carefully and cover the pan.
9. Add the coconut milk and soy sauce into the mixture.
10. Add the water into the mixture and cover the pan.
11. Let the soup cook for ten to fifteen minutes straight.
12. Add the chopped parsley, chopped cilantro, and sesame seeds on top.
13. Your dish is ready to be served.

## 1.9 Oyster Mushrooms in Rice Noodles Recipe

**Preparation Time:** 30 minutes
**Cooking Time:** 20 minutes
**Serving:** 4

**Ingredients:**

- One tablespoon hoisin sauce
- One tablespoon sriracha sauce
- Half cup sliced green onions
- One teaspoon rice wine
- One teaspoon fresh ginger
- One tablespoon fish sauce
- One tablespoon soy sauce
- One teaspoon Thai five spice
- Two tablespoon chili garlic sauce
- One cup of oyster mushrooms
- Half cup of fresh cilantro leaves
- A quarter cup of fresh basil leaves
- One teaspoon of chopped garlic
- Two tablespoon vegetable oil
- Dry noodles

**Instructions:**

1. Take a wok.
2. Add the hoisin sauce, sriracha sauce, chopped garlic, Thai spice, chili garlic sauce, and ginger into the wok.
3. Add the sauces into the wok mixture.
4. Cook the dish for ten minutes.
5. Add the mushrooms into the mixture.
6. Mix the mushrooms well and cook it for five minutes.
7. Cook the ingredients well and mix it with the rest of the ingredients.
8. Reduce the heat of the stove.
9. Add the dried noodles and water into the pan.
10. Add the rest of the ingredients into it.
11. Add the cilantro into the dish.
12. Mix the noodles and then dish them out.
13. Your dish is ready to be served.

## 1.10 Ginger and Coconut Rice Recipe

**Preparation Time:** 30 minutes
**Cooking Time:** 20 minutes
**Serving:** 4

**Ingredients:**

- One tablespoon hoisin sauce
- One tablespoon sriracha sauce
- Half cup sliced green onions
- One teaspoon rice wine
- Two teaspoons fresh ginger
- One tablespoon fish sauce
- One tablespoon soy sauce
- One teaspoon Thai five spice
- Two tablespoon chili garlic sauce
- One cup of desiccated coconut
- Half cup of fresh cilantro leaves
- A quarter cup of fresh basil leaves
- One teaspoon of chopped garlic
- Two tablespoon vegetable oil
- Cooked rice

**Instructions:**
1. Take a wok.
2. Add the hoisin sauce, sriracha sauce, chopped garlic, Thai spice, chili garlic sauce, and ginger into the wok.
3. Add the sauces into the wok mixture.
4. Cook the dish for ten minutes.
5. Add the coconut to the mixture.
6. Mix the mushrooms well and cook them for five minutes.
7. Cook the ingredients well and mix them with the rest of the ingredients.
8. Reduce the heat of the stove.
9. Add the cooked rice and water into the pan.
10. Add the rest of the ingredients into it.
11. Add the cilantro into the dish.
12. Mix the noodles and then dish them out.
13. Your dish is ready to be served.

## 1.11 Warm Egg and Potato Salad with Spicy Peanut Sauce Recipe

**Preparation Time:** 15 minutes
**Cooking Time:** 5 minutes
**Serving:** 4

**Ingredients:**

- Two tablespoons of sesame seeds
- One tablespoon of rice vinegar
- One teaspoon of sesame oil
- Four warm eggs
- Two tablespoons of white sugar
- Salt to taste
- Black pepper to taste
- A quarter cup of olive oil
- Two cups of boiled potato pieces
- One cup spicy peanut sauce
- One cup of chopped coriander

**Instructions:**
1. Take a skillet and add the sesame seeds into it.

2. Toast the seeds until they turn golden brown and fragrant.
3. Take a bowl and add the sesame oil, vinegar, olive oil, and sugar into it.
4. Add the peanut sauce, potatoes, and eggs into the bowl.
5. Mix all the ingredients well.
6. Top it with toasted sesame seeds.
7. Your dish is ready to be served.

## 1.12 Thai Quorn with Rive Recipe

**Preparation Time:** 30 minutes
**Cooking Time:** 20 minutes
**Serving:** 4

**Ingredients:**

- One tablespoon hoisin sauce
- One tablespoon sriracha sauce
- Half cup sliced green onions
- One teaspoon rice wine
- One teaspoon fresh ginger
- One tablespoon fish sauce
- One tablespoon soy sauce
- One teaspoon Thai five spice
- Two tablespoon chili garlic sauce
- One cup of quorn
- One cup of rice
- Half cup of fresh cilantro leaves
- A quarter cup of fresh basil leaves
- One teaspoon of chopped garlic
- Two tablespoon vegetable oil

**Instructions:**
1. Take a wok.
2. Add the hoisin sauce, sriracha sauce, chopped garlic, Thai spice, chili garlic sauce, and ginger into the wok.
3. Add the sauces into the wok mixture.
4. Cook the dish for ten minutes.
5. Add the quorn into the mixture.
6. Mix the quorn well and cook it for five minutes.
7. Cook the ingredients well and mix them with the rest of the ingredients.
8. Reduce the heat of the stove.
9. Add the cilantro into the dish.
10. Your dish is ready to be served.

## 1.13 Mango and Tofu Patties Recipe

**Preparation Time:** 15 minutes
**Cooking Time:** 15 minutes
**Serving:** 2

**Ingredients:**

- Oil
- Half cup of gram flour
- Two cups of chopped tofu
- Two cups of chopped onion
- A teaspoon of mix Thai spice powder
- Half tablespoon of chopped ginger
- Salt to taste
- Two cups of chopped mango

**Instructions:**
1. Take a large bowl.
2. Add the chopped tofu and mango into it.
3. Add the salt and pepper in it.
4. Add the chopped onions and mix spice powder.
5. Mix them well.
6. Add some oil to make dough of it.

7. Make round balls of the formed dough.
8. Add the gram flour and water into a bowl and make a paste.
9. Dip the balls in the paste.
10. Cook the balls on a hot pan full of oil.
11. Cook the patty well.
12. Your dish is ready to be served.

# 1.14 Creamy Roast Pepper Soup Recipe

**Preparation Time:** 10 minutes
**Cooking Time:** 30 minutes
**Serving:** 2

**Ingredients:**

- One pound roasted bell pepper
- Two tablespoons of olive oil
- Half cup of vegetable stock
- One cup of chopped tomatoes
- One cup of onion
- Three cups of water
- One tablespoon of soy sauce
- Salt to taste
- Black pepper to taste
- Chopped fresh cilantro leaves
- One cup of coconut cream
- Fresh parsley
- Toasted sesame seeds

**Instructions:**
1. Take a pan.

2. Add the oil and onions in it.
3. Cook the onions until they become soft and fragrant.
4. Add the chopped garlic into it.
5. Add the bell pepper pieces into the mixture.
6. Cook the mixture and add the tomatoes into it.
7. Add the bay leaves and some water in it.
8. Mix the ingredients carefully and cover the pan.
9. Add the coconut cream and soy sauce into the mixture.
10. Add the water into the mixture and cover the pan.
11. Let the soup cook for ten to fifteen minutes straight.
12. Add the chopped parsley, chopped cilantro, and sesame seeds on top.
13. Your dish is ready to be served.

## 1.15 Coconut and Pea Curry Recipe

**Preparation Time:** 30 minutes
**Cooking Time:** 30 minutes
**Serving:** 4

**Ingredients:**

- Two teaspoons of rice wine
- One teaspoon of caster sugar
- A quarter teaspoon of Sichuan pepper
- Two teaspoons of chopped red chili
- Half teaspoon of turmeric powder
- Black pepper to taste
- Salt to taste
- One tablespoon of chopped ginger
- One tablespoon of chopped garlic
- Half cup of finely chopped spring onions
- Two tablespoons of sesame oil
- Four teaspoons of dark soy sauce
- Two cups of peas
- One cup of coconut milk

**Instructions:**
1. Take a large pan.
2. Heat the oil in a pan and add the spring onions in it.
3. Cook it until they become soft and golden brown in color.
4. Add the chopped ginger and garlic into the pan.
5. Add the peas, rice wine and stir fry it until the color changes.
6. Cook the mixture well for about ten minutes until they are roasted.
7. Add coconut milk, caster sugar, white pepper, turmeric powder, red chili pepper, dark soy sauce, black pepper, and salt into the pan.
8. Add the rest of the ingredients into the mixture.
9. Cook the ingredients well for about fifteen to twenty minutes.
10. Your dish is ready to be served.

## 1.16 Mix Mushroom and Vegetable Salad Recipe

**Preparation Time:** 15 minutes
**Cooking Time:** 5 minutes
**Serving:** 4

### Ingredients:

- Two tablespoons of sesame seeds
- One tablespoon of rice vinegar
- One teaspoon of sesame oil
- Two tablespoons of white sugar
- Salt to taste
- Black pepper to taste
- A quarter cup of olive oil
- Two cups of mixed vegetables
- One cup of mixed mushrooms

### Instructions:
1. Take a skillet and add the sesame seeds into it.
2. Toast the seeds until they turn golden brown and fragrant.
3. Take a bowl and add the sesame oil, vinegar, olive oil, and sugar into it.

4. Add the vegetables and mushrooms into the bowl.
5. Mix all the ingredients well.
6. Top it with toasted sesame seeds.
7. Your dish is ready to be served.

# 1.17 Thai Lemongrass and Tofu Curry Recipe

**Preparation Time:** 30 minutes
**Cooking Time:** 30 minutes
**Serving:** 4

**Ingredients:**

- Two teaspoons of rice wine
- One teaspoon of caster sugar
- A quarter teaspoon of Sichuan pepper
- Two teaspoons of chopped red chili
- Half teaspoon of turmeric powder
- Black pepper to taste
- Salt to taste
- One tablespoon of chopped ginger
- One tablespoon of chopped garlic
- Half cup of finely chopped spring onions
- Two tablespoons of sesame oil
- Four teaspoons of dark soy sauce
- Two cups of tofu
- Two teaspoons of dried lemongrass
- One cup of coconut milk

**Instructions:**
1. Take a large pan.
2. Heat the oil in a pan and add the spring onions in it.
3. Cook it until they become soft and golden brown in color.
4. Add the chopped ginger and garlic into the pan.
5. Add the tofu, rice wine and stir fry it until the color changes.
6. Cook the mixture well for about ten minutes until they are roasted.
7. Add coconut milk, caster sugar, lemongrass, white pepper, turmeric powder, red chili pepper, dark soy sauce, black pepper, and salt into the pan.
8. Add the rest of the ingredients into the mixture.
9. Cook the ingredients well for about fifteen to twenty minutes.
10. Your dish is ready to be served.

## 1.18 Thai Peanut and Mango Salad Recipe

**Preparation Time:** 15 minutes
**Cooking Time:** 5 minutes
**Serving:** 4

**Ingredients:**

- Two tablespoons of sesame seeds
- One tablespoon of rice vinegar
- One teaspoon of sesame oil
- Two tablespoons of white sugar
- Salt to taste
- Black pepper to taste
- A quarter cup of olive oil
- Two cups of peanuts
- One cup of mangoes

**Instructions:**
1. Take a skillet and add the sesame seeds into it.
2. Toast the seeds until they turn golden brown and fragrant.
3. Take a bowl and add the sesame oil, vinegar, olive oil, and sugar into it.
4. Add the peanuts and mango into the bowl.

5. Mix all the ingredients well.
6. Top it with toasted sesame seeds.
7. Your dish is ready to be served.

## 1.19 Spicy Thai Green Papaya Soup Recipe

**Preparation Time:** 10 minutes
**Cooking Time:** 30 minutes
**Serving:** 2

**Ingredients:**

- One pound green papaya
- Two tablespoons of green curry paste
- Two tablespoons of olive oil
- Half cup of vegetable stock
- One cup of chopped tomatoes
- One cup of onion
- Three cups of water
- One tablespoon of soy sauce
- Salt to taste
- Black pepper to taste
- Chopped fresh cilantro leaves
- One cup of coconut milk
- Fresh parsley
- Toasted sesame seeds

**Instructions:**
1. Take a pan.
2. Add the oil and onions in it.
3. Cook the onions until they become soft and fragrant.
4. Add the chopped garlic into it.
5. Add the papaya pieces into the mixture.
6. Cook the mixture and add the tomatoes into it.
7. Add the bay leaves, green curry paste, and some water in it.
8. Mix the ingredients carefully and cover the pan.
9. Add the coconut milk and soy sauce into the mixture.
10. Add the water into the mixture and cover the pan.
11. Let the soup cook for ten to fifteen minutes straight.
12. Add the chopped parsley, chopped cilantro, and sesame seeds on top.
13. Your dish is ready to be served.

## 1.20 Spicy Thai Bean Fritters Recipe

**Preparation Time:** 20 minutes
**Cooking Time:** 20 minutes
**Serving:** 4

**Ingredients:**

- Cooking oil
- One cup of gram flour
- One cup of parboiled beans
- Two tablespoons of mix Thai spice
- One cup of chopped tomatoes

**Instructions:**
1. Take a large bowl.
2. Add all the things into the bowl except the cooking oil.
3. Mix all the ingredients well and add water into the mixture to form a semi-thick batter.
4. Add the oil into a large frying pan.
5. Heat the oil and then add the mixture a little at a time with the help of a spoon.
6. Cook the fritters until they turn golden brown.
7. The dish is ready to be served.

# Chapter 2: Vegetarian Chinese Recipes

Chinese are incredibly fond of vegetables in each meal. Following are some amazing Chinese recipes that you will love to make:

## 2.1 Chinese Green Bean Chow Mein Recipe

**Preparation Time:** 30 minutes
**Cooking Time:** 10 minutes
**Serving:** 4

**Ingredients:**

- Two red chilies
- Two teaspoons of chopped celery
- Half cup of sliced green onions
- One teaspoon of white peppercorns
- One teaspoon of fresh ginger
- One tablespoon of fish sauce
- One tablespoon of soy sauce
- Half teaspoon of Chinese five-spice
- Two tablespoons of chili garlic sauce
- Half cup of bamboo shoots
- Fresh cilantro leaves
- Fresh basil leaves

- Two cups of green beans
- Two cups of vegetable broth
- One teaspoon of chopped garlic
- Two tablespoons of sesame oil
- Egg noodles

**Instructions:**
1. Take a wok.
2. Add the white peppercorns, chopped garlic, Chinese five-spice, red chilies, basil leaves, and ginger into the wok.
3. Add the vegetable broth and sauces into the wok mixture.
4. Cook the dish for ten minutes.
5. Add the green beans into the mixture.
6. Mix the vegetables well and cook them for five minutes.
7. Reduce the heat of the stove.
8. Boil the egg noodles according to the instructions on the pack.
9. Drain the noodles when done, and then add them into the pan.
10. Add the rest of the ingredients into it.
11. Cook the dish for five more minutes.
12. Add the cilantro into the dish.
13. Your dish is ready to be served.

## 2.2 Chinese General Tso Tofu Recipe

**Preparation Time:** 5 minutes
**Cooking Time:** 20 minutes
**Serving:** 4

**Ingredients:**

- One pound of tofu pieces
- Two cups of corn flakes
- Two eggs
- Cooking spray
- Two garlic cloves
- One cup of vegetable broth
- One teaspoon of sriracha sauce
- One tablespoon of Dijon mustard
- Two tablespoons of vinegar
- A pinch of salt
- A pinch of black pepper

**Instructions:**
1. Take a bowl.
2. Add the eggs into the bowl and mix well.
3. Dip the tofu pieces in the egg mixture and then coat with corn flakes.

4. Add the cooking spray on top and bake the tofu pieces
5. Add the rest of the ingredients into the bowl.
6. Mix well.
7. Add the rest of the ingredients into a pan and cook.
8. Cook well to get a thick and homogenized mixture.
9. Dish out the tofu pieces when done, and then dump them into the prepared sauce.
10. Bake the tofu pieces again for ten minutes.
11. Your dish is ready to be served.

## 2.3 Chinese Fried Okra Salad Recipe

**Preparation Time:** 15 minutes
**Cooking Time:** 5 minutes
**Serving:** 4

### Ingredients:

- Two tablespoons of sesame seeds
- One tablespoon of rice vinegar
- One teaspoon of sesame oil
- Two tablespoons of white sugar
- Salt
- Black pepper
- Two cups of fried okra
- Chopped fresh cilantro

### Instructions:
1. Take a skillet and add the sesame seeds into it.
2. Toast the seeds until they become golden brown and fragrant.
3. Take a bowl and add the sesame oil, vinegar, olive oil, and sugar into it.
4. Add the fried okra into the bowl.
5. Mix all the ingredients well.

6. Top it with toasted sesame seeds.
7. Garnish it with chopped fresh cilantro.
8. Your dish is ready to be served.

## 2.4 Spiced Cashew Vegetables Recipe

**Preparation Time:** 30 minutes
**Cooking Time:** 10 minutes
**Serving:** 4

**Ingredients:**

- One teaspoon of white peppercorns
- One teaspoon of fresh ginger
- One tablespoon of fish sauce
- One tablespoon of soy sauce
- Half teaspoon of Chinese five-spice
- Two tablespoons of chili garlic sauce
- One cup of Chinese red chili
- One teaspoon of sesame seeds
- One teaspoon of chopped garlic
- Two teaspoons of sesame oil
- One cup of cashews
- Two cups of vegetables

**Instructions:**
1. Take a wok.

2. Add the white peppercorns, chopped garlic, Chinese five-spice, red chilies, and ginger into the wok.
3. Take a non-stick frying pan.
4. Add the cashews and vegetables into the pan.
5. Cook the ingredients and dish them out.
6. Add the sauces into the wok mixture.
7. Cook the dish for ten minutes.
8. Add the cashews, vegetables and cook it for five minutes.
9. Mix the rest of the ingredients into it.
10. Cook the dish for five more minutes.
11. Your dish is ready to be served.

## 2.5 Spiced Mushroom Dumplings Recipe

**Preparation Time:** 50 minutes
**Cooking Time:** 30 minutes
**Serving:** 4

**Ingredients:**

- Half cup of mushrooms
- One tablespoon of thin soy sauce
- Half teaspoon of cinnamon powder
- One tablespoon of sweet vinegar
- One tablespoon of Chinese five-spice powder
- Half tablespoon of fresh shallot
- Four green chilies
- One cup of milk
- One tablespoon of vegetable oil
- One cup of all-purpose flour
- Half cup of whole wheat flour
- A pinch of salt
- Half cup of chopped chives

**Instructions:**
1. Take a bowl and add the flour into it.
2. Add lukewarm water in it.
3. Set aside for half-hour.
4. Take the whole wheat flour.
5. Add the salt and some milk in it.
6. Combine the ingredients to form a soft dough.
7. Knee it for ten minutes.
8. Make small balls from the dough.
9. Take a small bowl.
10. Add the mushrooms, green chilies, chives, and the rest of the ingredients.
11. Add the formed mixture into the round dough with the help of the oil.
12. Steam the dumplings in a water bath for ten minutes.
13. Take out the dumplings when done.
14. Your dish is ready to be served.

## 2.6 Vegetarian Tofu Wonton Recipe

**Preparation Time:** 10 minutes
**Cooking Time:** 20 minutes
**Serving:** 4

### Ingredients:

- Two tablespoons of sesame oil
- One tablespoon of red pepper flakes
- One cup of chopped tofu
- Three garlic cloves
- Three diced shallots
- Half teaspoon of kosher salt
- One teaspoon of black pepper
- One tablespoon of chopped parsley
- Wonton wrappers
- Oil

### Instructions:

1. Take a saucepan and add the oil in it.
2. Heat the oil and add all the filling ingredients into it.
3. Cook it for few minutes.

4. Cock it until the mixture becomes fragrant.
5. Your filling is ready.
6. Take the wonton wrappers and place the filling there and fold them carefully.
7. Add oil into a frying pan.
8. Fry the wontons well until they turn light brown.
9. Dish out when the wontons are done.
10. Your dish is ready to be served.

## 2.7 Honey Chili Potatoes Recipe

**Preparation Time:** 5 minutes
**Cooking Time:** 20 minutes
**Serving:** 4

**Ingredients:**

- One pound of potatoes
- Two eggs
- Cooking spray
- Two teaspoons of sesame seeds
- One cup of vegetable broth
- One teaspoon of hot sauce
- One tablespoon of honey
- Two tablespoons of vinegar
- A pinch of salt
- A pinch of black pepper

**Instructions:**
1. Take a bowl.
2. Add the eggs into the bowl and mix well.
3. Dip the potatoes in the egg mixture.

4. Add the cooking spray on top and bake the beef ribs.
5. Add the rest of the ingredients into the bowl.
6. Mix well.
7. Add the rest of the ingredients into a pan and cook.
8. Cook well to get a thick and homogenized mixture.
9. Dish out the potatoes when done and then dump them into the prepared sauce.
10. Bake the potatoes again for ten minutes.
11. Your dish is ready to be served.

## 2.8 Shitake Fried Rice Recipe

**Preparation Time:** 30 minutes
**Cooking Time:** 10 minutes
**Serving:** 4

**Ingredients:**

- Half cup of sliced green onions
- One teaspoon of white peppercorns
- One teaspoon of fresh ginger
- One tablespoon of fish sauce
- One tablespoon of soy sauce
- Half teaspoon of Chinese five-spice
- Two tablespoons of chili garlic sauce
- One cup of vegetable broth
- One teaspoon of minced lemongrass
- One teaspoon of chopped garlic
- Two teaspoons of sesame oil
- One cup of shitake mushrooms
- Cooked rice

**Instructions:**
1. Take a wok.

2. Add the minced lemongrass, white peppercorns, chopped garlic, Chinese five-spice, red chilies, basil leaves, and ginger into the wok.
3. Take a non-stick frying pan.
4. Add the mushrooms into the pan.
5. Cook the mushrooms and dish them out.
6. Add the vegetable broth and sauces into the wok mixture.
7. Cook the dish for ten minutes.
8. Add the cooked rice into the mixture.
9. Mix the rice well and cook it for five minutes.
10. Add the mushrooms and then mix the rest of the ingredients into it.
11. Cook the dish for five more minutes.
12. Your dish is ready to be served.

## 2.9 Vegetable Manchow Soup Recipe

**Preparation Time:** 30 minutes
**Cooking Time:** 10 minutes
**Serving:** 4

**Ingredients:**

- Two cups of chopped mixed vegetables
- Two tablespoons of minced garlic
- Two tablespoons of minced ginger
- Half cup of cilantro
- Two tablespoons of sesame oil
- Two tablespoons of cornflour
- Half cup of water
- Two cups of vegetable stock
- One cup of water
- Two cups of rice noodles
- One cup of chopped tomatoes
- One teaspoon of Chinese five-spice powder
- One cup of onion
- Half teaspoon of Chinese paprika

**Instructions:**
1. Take a pan.
2. Add in the oil and onions.
3. Cook the onions until they become soft and fragrant.
4. Add in the chopped garlic and ginger.
5. Cook the mixture and add the tomatoes into it.
6. Add the spices and sauces.
7. Add the vegetables and noodles into it when the tomatoes are done.
8. Add in the vegetable broth and water.
9. Add the cornflour and the rest of the ingredients except the cilantro.
10. Mix the ingredients carefully and cover the pan.
11. Add cilantro on top.
12. Your dish is ready to be served.

## 2.10 Vegetable Chopsuey Recipe

**Preparation Time:** 30 minutes
**Cooking Time:** 10 minutes
**Serving:** 4

**Ingredients:**

- Two red chilies
- Half cup of sliced green onions
- One teaspoon of white peppercorns
- One teaspoon of fresh ginger
- Half teaspoon of Chinese five-spice
- Fresh cilantro leaves
- Fresh basil leaves
- Two cups of chopped vegetables
- Two cups of vegetable broth
- One teaspoon of chopped garlic
- Two tablespoons of sesame oil
- Egg noodles

**Instructions:**
1. Take a wok.

2. Add the white peppercorns, chopped garlic, Chinese five-spice, red chilies, basil leaves, and ginger into the wok.
3. Add the vegetable broth into the wok mixture.
4. Cook the dish for ten minutes.
5. Add the vegetables into the mixture.
6. Mix the vegetables well and cook them for five minutes.
7. Reduce the heat of the stove.
8. Boil the egg noodles according to the instructions on the pack.
9. Drain the noodles when done, and then add them into the pan.
10. Add the rest of the ingredients into it.
11. Cook the dish for five more minutes.
12. Add the cilantro into the dish.
13. Your dish is ready to be served.

## 2.11 Vegetarian Hakka Noodles Recipe

**Preparation Time:** 30 minutes
**Cooking Time:** 10 minutes
**Serving:** 4

**Ingredients:**

- Two red chilies
- Half cup of sliced green onions
- One teaspoon of white peppercorns
- One teaspoon of fresh ginger
- One tablespoon of fish sauce
- One tablespoon of soy sauce
- Half teaspoon of Chinese five-spice
- Two tablespoons of chili garlic sauce
- Fresh cilantro leaves
- Fresh basil leaves
- Two cups of chopped vegetables
- Two cups of vegetable broth
- One teaspoon of chopped garlic
- Two tablespoons of sesame oil
- Egg noodles

**Instructions:**
1. Take a wok.
2. Add the white peppercorns, chopped garlic, Chinese five-spice, red chilies, basil leaves, and ginger into the wok.
3. Add the vegetable broth and sauces into the wok mixture.
4. Cook the dish for ten minutes.
5. Add the vegetables into the mixture.
6. Mix the vegetables well and cook them for five minutes.
7. Reduce the heat of the stove.
8. Boil the egg noodles according to the instructions on the pack.
9. Drain the noodles when done, and then add them into the pan.
10. Add the rest of the ingredients into it.
11. Cook the dish for five more minutes.
12. Add the cilantro into the dish.
13. Your dish is ready to be served.

## 2.12 Chili Paneer Dry Recipe

**Preparation Time:** 30 minutes
**Cooking Time:** 10 minutes
**Serving:** 4

**Ingredients:**

- One teaspoon of white peppercorns
- One teaspoon of fresh ginger
- One tablespoon of fish sauce
- One tablespoon of soy sauce
- Half teaspoon of Chinese five-spice
- Two tablespoons of chili garlic sauce
- One cup of Chinese red chili
- One teaspoon of minced lemongrass
- One teaspoon of chopped garlic
- Two teaspoons of sesame oil
- One cup of tofu chunks

**Instructions:**
1. Take a wok.

2. Add the minced lemongrass, white peppercorns, chopped garlic, Chinese five-spice, red chilies, basil leaves, and ginger into the wok.
3. Take a non-stick frying pan.
4. Add the tofu into the pan.
5. Cook the ingredients and dish them out.
6. Add the vegetable broth and sauces into the wok mixture.
7. Cook the dish for ten minutes.
8. Add the tofu and cook it for five minutes.
9. Mix the rest of the ingredients into it.
10. Cook the dish for five more minutes.
11. Your dish is ready to be served.

## 2.13 Crunchy Iceberg Dumplings Recipe

**Preparation Time:** 50 minutes
**Cooking Time:** 30 minutes
**Serving:** 4

**Ingredients:**

- Half cup of iceberg
- One tablespoon of thin soy sauce
- Half teaspoon of cinnamon powder
- One tablespoon of sweet vinegar
- One tablespoon of Chinese five-spice powder
- Half tablespoon of fresh shallot
- Four green chilies
- One cup of milk
- One tablespoon of vegetable oil
- One cup of all-purpose flour
- Half cup of whole wheat flour
- A pinch of salt
- Half cup of chopped chives

**Instructions:**
1. Take a bowl and add the flour into it.
2. Add lukewarm water in it.
3. Set aside for half-hour.
4. Take the whole wheat flour.
5. Add the salt and some milk in it.
6. Combine the ingredients to form a soft dough.
7. Knee it for ten minutes.
8. Make small balls from the dough.
9. Take a small bowl.
10. Add the iceberg, green chilies, chives, and the rest of the ingredients.
11. Add the formed mixture into the round dough with the help of the oil.
12. Steam the dumplings in a water bath for ten minutes.
13. Take out the dumplings when done.
14. Your dish is ready to be served.

## 2.14 Chestnut Fried Rice Recipe

**Preparation Time:** 30 minutes
**Cooking Time:** 10 minutes
**Serving:** 4

**Ingredients:**

- Half cup of sliced green onions
- One teaspoon of white peppercorns
- One teaspoon of fresh ginger
- One tablespoon of fish sauce
- One tablespoon of soy sauce
- Half teaspoon of Chinese five-spice
- Two tablespoons of chili garlic sauce
- One cup of vegetable broth
- One teaspoon of minced lemongrass
- One teaspoon of chopped garlic
- Two teaspoons of sesame oil
- One cup of sliced chestnuts
- Cooked rice

**Instructions:**
1. Take a wok.

2. Add the minced lemongrass, white peppercorns, chopped garlic, Chinese five-spice, red chilies, basil leaves, and ginger into the wok.
3. Take a non-stick frying pan.
4. Add the chestnuts into the pan.
5. Cook the chestnuts and dish them out.
6. Add the vegetable broth and sauces into the wok mixture.
7. Cook the dish for ten minutes.
8. Add the cooked rice into the mixture.
9. Mix the rice well and cook it for five minutes.
10. Add the chestnuts and then mix the rest of the ingredients into it.
11. Cook the dish for five more minutes.
12. Your dish is ready to be served.

## 2.15 Chili and Garlic Noodles Recipe

**Preparation Time:** 30 minutes
**Cooking Time:** 10 minutes
**Serving:** 4

**Ingredients:**

- One teaspoon of white peppercorns
- One teaspoon of fresh ginger
- One tablespoon of fish sauce
- One tablespoon of soy sauce
- Half teaspoon of Chinese five-spice
- Two tablespoons of chili garlic sauce
- One cup of Chinese red chili
- One teaspoon of minced lemongrass
- One teaspoon of chopped garlic
- Two teaspoons of sesame oil
- One cup of egg noodles

**Instructions:**
1. Take a wok.

2. Add the minced lemongrass, white peppercorns, chopped garlic, Chinese five-spice, red chilies, basil leaves, and ginger into the wok.
3. Add the vegetable broth and sauces into the wok mixture.
4. Cook the dish for ten minutes.
5. Add the noodles and cook them for five minutes.
6. Mix the rest of the ingredients into it.
7. Cook the dish for five more minutes.
8. Your dish is ready to be served.

## 2.16 Ricotta Wontons Recipe

**Preparation Time:** 10 minutes
**Cooking Time:** 20 minutes
**Serving:** 4

**Ingredients:**

- Two tablespoons of sesame oil
- One tablespoon of red pepper flakes
- One cup of chopped ricotta cheese
- Three garlic cloves
- Three diced shallots
- Half teaspoon of kosher salt
- One teaspoon of black pepper
- One tablespoon of chopped parsley
- Wonton wrappers
- Oil

**Instructions:**
1. Take a saucepan and add the oil in it.
2. Heat the oil and add all the filling ingredients into it.
3. Cook it for few minutes.

4. Cook it until the mixture becomes fragrant.
5. Your filling is ready.
6. Take the wonton wrappers and place the filling there and fold them carefully.
7. Add oil into a frying pan.
8. Fry the wontons well until they turn light brown.
9. Dish out when the wontons are done.
10. Your dish is ready to be served.

## 2.17 Spiced Tofu Hotpot Recipe

**Preparation Time:** 20 minutes
**Cooking Time:** 20 minutes
**Serving:** 4

**Ingredients:**

- One tablespoon of oyster sauce
- Four Chinese chili peppers
- One tablespoon of fish sauce
- Half tablespoon of soy sauce
- Two teaspoons of minced garlic
- Three tablespoons of cooking oil
- Half cup of hot sauce
- Two cups of tofu cubes
- Salt as needed
- Chopped fresh cilantro for garnishing

**Instructions:**
1. Take a large pan.
2. Add the cooking oil into the pan and heat it.
3. Add the tofu into the pan and stir-fry it.
4. Add the minced garlic into the pan.

5. Add the soy sauce, fish sauce, Chinese chili peppers, hot sauce, and rest of the ingredients into the mixture.
6. Cook the dish for ten minutes and add some water for curry.
7. Dish out the tofu and garnish it with chopped fresh cilantro leaves.
8. Your dish is ready to be served.

## 2.18 Oyster and Spinach Stir-Fry Recipe

**Preparation Time:** 30 minutes
**Cooking Time:** 30 minutes
**Serving:** 4

**Ingredients:**

- Two teaspoons of rice wine
- Two cups of spinach
- A quarter teaspoon of Sichuan pepper
- Two teaspoons of chopped red chili
- One cup of oyster sauce
- Black pepper
- Salt
- One tablespoon of chopped ginger
- One tablespoon of chopped garlic
- Two tablespoons of sesame oil
- Four teaspoons of dark soy sauce

**Instructions:**
1. Take a large pan.
2. Heat the oil in a pan.
3. Add the chopped ginger and garlic into the pan.

4. Add the oyster sauce and spinach in the pan.
5. Cook the mixture well for about ten minutes until they are roasted.
6. Add caster sugar, Sichuan pepper, red chili pepper, dark soy sauce, black pepper, and salt into the pan.
7. Cook the ingredients well for about fifteen minutes.
8. Your dish is ready to be served.

## 2.19 Spiced Chickpea Stir-Fry Recipe

**Preparation Time:** 30 minutes
**Cooking Time:** 30 minutes
**Serving:** 4

**Ingredients:**

- Two teaspoons of rice wine
- Two cups of chickpeas
- A quarter teaspoon of Sichuan pepper
- Two teaspoons of chopped red chili
- One cup of chili garlic sauce
- Black pepper
- Salt
- One tablespoon of chopped ginger
- One tablespoon of chopped garlic
- Two tablespoons of sesame oil
- Four teaspoons of dark soy sauce

**Instructions:**
1. Take a large pan.
2. Heat the oil in a pan.
3. Add the chopped ginger and garlic into the pan.

4. Add the rice wine and chickpeas in the pan.
5. Cook the mixture well for about ten minutes until they are roasted.
6. Add caster sugar, Sichuan pepper, red chili pepper, dark soy sauce, black pepper and salt into the pan.
7. Add the chili garlic sauce into the mixture.
8. Cook the ingredients well for about fifteen minutes.
9. Your dish is ready to be served.

## 2.20 Carrot Dumplings Recipe

**Preparation Time:** 50 minutes
**Cooking Time:** 30 minutes
**Serving:** 4

**Ingredients:**

- Half cup of carrots
- One tablespoon of thin soy sauce
- Half teaspoon of cinnamon powder
- One tablespoon of sweet vinegar
- One tablespoon of Chinese five-spice powder
- Half tablespoon of fresh shallot
- Four green chilies
- One cup of milk
- One tablespoon of vegetable oil
- One cup of all-purpose flour
- Half cup of whole wheat flour
- A pinch of salt
- Half cup of chopped chives

**Instructions:**
1. Take a bowl and add the flour into it.
2. Add lukewarm water in it.
3. Set aside for half-hour.
4. Take the whole wheat flour.
5. Add the salt and some milk in it.
6. Combine the ingredients to form a soft dough.
7. Knee it for ten minutes.
8. Make small balls from the dough.
9. Take a small bowl.
10. Add the carrots, green chilies, chives, and rest of the ingredients.
11. Add the formed mixture into the round dough with the help of the oil.
12. Steam the dumplings in a water bath for ten minutes.
13. Take out the dumplings when done.
14. Your dish is ready to be served.

# Chapter 3: Vegetarian Japanese Recipes

Vegetarian Japanese recipes are extremely healthy and loved by people everywhere in the world. Following are some classic Japanese recipes that are rich in healthy nutrients, and you can easily make them with the detailed instructions listed in each recipe:

## 3.1 Creamy Asparagus Pasta Recipe

**Preparation Time:** 30 minutes
**Cooking Time:** 10 minutes
**Serving:** 4

**Ingredients:**

- Two tablespoons of minced ginger
- Half cup of cilantro
- Two tablespoons of olive oil
- One cup of chopped tomatoes
- One pack of pasta
- One cup of vegetable broth
- One cup of onion
- One tablespoon of miso paste
- Half cup of heavy cream
- One teaspoon of Japanese mixed spice

- One cup of chopped asparagus
- Two tablespoons of minced garlic

**Instructions:**
1. Boil the pasta according to the instructions on the package.
2. Drain the pasta.
3. Take a pan.
4. Add in the oil and onions.
5. Cook the onions until they become soft and fragrant.
6. Add in the chopped garlic and ginger.
7. Add the spices and tomatoes.
8. Add in the broth and miso paste.
9. Mix the ingredients carefully and cover the pan.
10. Add the asparagus into the mixture.
11. Mix the pasta into the mixture.
12. Add the heavy cream in the end.
13. Add cilantro on top.
14. Your dish is ready to be served.

## 3.2 Teriyaki Sauce Vegetables Recipe

**Preparation Time:** 30 minutes
**Cooking Time:** 20 minutes
**Serving:** 4

**Ingredients:**

- Half cup of carrot cubes
- Two cups of red bell pepper cubes
- One cup of zucchini cubes
- One cup of broccoli florets
- One cup of Japanese eggplant
- One tablespoon of corn starch
- One cup of teriyaki sauce
- Cooking oil

**Instructions:**
1. Take a large pan.
2. Add the vegetables and oil into the pan.
3. Stir-fry the vegetables.
4. Add all the rest of the ingredients.
5. Dish out the ingredients when done.
6. Your dish is ready to be served.

## 3.3 Vegetarian Soufflé Pancakes Recipe

**Preparation Time:** 10 minutes
**Cooking Time:** 30 minutes
**Serving:** 4

**Ingredients:**

- Two eggs
- One tablespoon of matcha powder
- One tablespoon of maple syrup
- Half cup of coconut milk
- Half cup of white sugar
- A pinch of salt
- One tablespoon of vanilla extract
- Two cups of cake flour
- One cup of butter

**Instructions:**
1. Take a medium bowl and add the eggs, matcha powder, and cake flour to it.
2. Add one cup of coconut milk and mix well.
3. Add the sugar, the salt and the beaten eggs.
4. Mix them well.

5. Add the baking soda in the mixture.
6. Add the maple syrup into it.
7. Mix it for few minutes.
8. Bake the cake for twenty to twenty-five minutes.
9. Your dish is ready to be served.

## 3.4 Japanese Miso Rice Recipe

**Preparation Time:** 30 minutes
**Cooking Time:** 10 minutes
**Serving:** 4

**Ingredients:**

- One teaspoon of dashi powder
- One cup of sliced green onions
- One teaspoon of white miso paste
- One cup of cilantro
- One teaspoon of fresh ginger
- One tablespoon of mirin paste
- One tablespoon of soy sauce
- Two tablespoons of oyster sauce
- Cooked rice

**Instructions:**
1. Heat a large pan.
2. Add all the ingredients except the green onions and rice.
3. Cook the dish for ten minutes.
4. Add the green onions into the mixture.

5. Mix the green onions well and cook them for five minutes.
6. Add the rest of the ingredients into the mixture.
7. Cook the rice for five more minutes.
8. Your dish is ready to be served.

## 3.5 Kabocha Soup Recipe

**Preparation Time:** 30 minutes
**Cooking Time:** 20 minutes
**Serving:** 4

**Ingredients:**

- One cup of kabocha
- One teaspoon of miso paste
- One cup of onion
- One cup of bell peppers
- One cup of water
- Two tablespoons of minced garlic
- Two tablespoons of minced ginger
- Half cup of cilantro
- One cup of diced carrots
- Two tablespoons of olive oil
- One cup of vegetable stock
- One cup of chopped tomatoes

**Instructions:**
1. Take a pan.
2. Add in the oil and onions.

3. Cook the onions until they become soft and fragrant.
4. Add in the chopped garlic and ginger.
5. Cook the mixture and add the tomatoes into it.
6. Add the spices.
7. Add the kabocha and miso paste into it.
8. Mix the ingredients carefully and cover the pan.
9. Add the vegetables and the rest of the ingredients.
10. Add the water into the mixture and let the mixture boil.
11. Let the soup cook for ten to fifteen minutes straight.
12. Add cilantro on top.
13. Your dish is ready to be served.

## 3.6 Miso Vegetable Curry Recipe

**Preparation Time:** 30 minutes
**Cooking Time:** 10 minutes
**Serving:** 4

**Ingredients:**

- Half cup of cilantro
- Two tablespoons of sesame oil
- One cup of chopped tomatoes
- One cup of lemon juice
- One tablespoon of powdered cumin
- Salt to taste
- Black pepper to taste
- One teaspoon of miso paste
- One cup of onion
- One cup of vegetable broth
- Half teaspoon of cornstarch
- Two cups of mixed vegetables
- Two tablespoons of minced garlic
- Two tablespoons of minced ginger

**Instructions:**
1. Take a pan.
2. Add in the oil and onions.
3. Cook the onions until they become soft and fragrant.
4. Add in the chopped garlic and ginger.
5. Cook the mixture and add the tomatoes into it.
6. Add the spices.
7. Add the vegetables into it.
8. Cook for five minutes.
9. Add in the broth and the rest of the ingredients.
10. Add the cornstarch into the mixture.
11. Garnish the dish with chopped cilantro leaves
12. Your dish is ready to be served.

## 3.7 Teriyaki Tofu Dry Recipe

**Preparation Time:** 30 minutes
**Cooking Time:** 10 minutes
**Serving:** 4

**Ingredients:**

- One teaspoon of fresh ginger
- One tablespoon of fish sauce
- One tablespoon of soy sauce
- Half teaspoon of Japanese five spice
- Two tablespoons of chili garlic sauce
- One cup of teriyaki sauce
- One teaspoon of chopped garlic
- Two teaspoons of sesame oil
- One cup of tofu chunks

**Instructions:**
1. Take a wok.
2. Add the chopped garlic, Japanese five-spice, red chilies, basil leaves, and ginger into the wok.
3. Take a non-stick frying pan.
4. Add the tofu into the pan.

5. Cook the ingredients and dish them out.
6. Add the vegetable broth and sauces into the wok mixture.
7. Cook the dish for ten minutes.
8. Add the tofu and cook it for five minutes.
9. Mix the rest of the ingredients into it.
10. Cook the dish for five more minutes.
11. Your dish is ready to be served.

## 3.8 Inari Tofu Recipe

**Preparation Time:** 10 minutes
**Cooking Time:** 20 minutes
**Serving:** 4

### Ingredients:

- Half pound of tofu
- One shredded cabbage
- Half cup of mayonnaise
- Salt to taste
- Black pepper to taste
- Two cups of inari
- Half cup of spring onions

### Instructions:
1. Add all the ingredients into a bowl except the tuna.
2. Mix all the ingredients well.
3. Lay the tofu pieces and add the formed mixture on top.
4. Roll the tofu and cut it into pieces.
5. Your dish is ready to be served.

## 3.9 Spicy Soba Soup Recipe

**Preparation Time:** 30 minutes
**Cooking Time:** 20 minutes
**Serving:** 4

**Ingredients:**

- One cup of soba noodles
- One teaspoon of miso paste
- One cup of onion
- One cup of water
- Two tablespoons of minced garlic
- Two tablespoons of minced ginger
- Half cup of cilantro
- One cup of diced carrots
- Two tablespoons of chili paste
- Two tablespoons of olive oil
- One cup of vegetable stock
- One cup of chopped tomatoes

**Instructions:**
1. Take a pan.
2. Add in the oil and onions.

3. Cook the onions until they become soft and fragrant.
4. Add in the chopped garlic and ginger.
5. Cook the mixture and add the tomatoes into it.
6. Add the spices.
7. Add the soba noodles and miso paste into it.
8. Mix the ingredients carefully and cover the pan.
9. Add the rest of the ingredients.
10. Add the water into the mixture and let the mixture boil.
11. Let the soup cook for ten to fifteen minutes straight.
12. Add cilantro on top.
13. Your dish is ready to be served.

## 3.10 Mashed Green Beans and Tofu Salad Recipe

**Preparation Time:** 10 minutes
**Cooking Time:** 20 minutes
**Serving:** 4

**Ingredients:**

- One cup of mashed green beans
- One tablespoon of sesame oil
- One tablespoon of rice vinegar
- One tablespoon of ginger
- One tablespoon of garlic powder
- One cup of spring onions
- One tablespoon of sesame seeds
- One teaspoon of soy sauce
- One cup of chopped tofu
- Salt, to taste
- Pepper, to taste

**Instructions:**
1. Take a large bowl and add the green beans into it.
2. Add the ginger and garlic powder.

3. Mix well.
4. Add the sesame oil and rice vinegar into it.
5. Add the spring onions, Japanese red chili, and soy sauce.
6. Add the salt and pepper as you like.
7. Add the sesame seeds and mix well so that a homogeneous mixture is obtained.
8. Add the tofu into the mixture.
9. Mix all ingredients and make a good combination.
10. Your salad is ready to be served.

## 3.11 Spicy Eggplant Donburi Recipe

**Preparation Time:** 30 minutes
**Cooking Time:** 10 minutes
**Serving:** 4

**Ingredients:**

- Half cup of cilantro
- Two tablespoons of sesame oil
- One cup of chopped tomatoes
- One cup of lemon juice
- One tablespoon of powdered cumin
- Salt to taste
- Black pepper to taste
- One teaspoon of chili paste
- One cup of onion
- One cup of vegetable broth
- Half teaspoon of cornstarch
- Two cups of eggplant pieces
- Two tablespoons of minced garlic
- Two tablespoons of minced ginger

**Instructions:**
1. Take a pan.
2. Add in the oil and onions.
3. Cook the onions until they become soft and fragrant.
4. Add in the chopped garlic and ginger.
5. Cook the mixture and add the tomatoes into it.
6. Add the spices.
7. Add the eggplant pieces into it.
8. Cook for five minutes.
9. Add in the broth and the rest of the ingredients.
10. Add the cornstarch into the mixture.
11. Garnish the dish with chopped cilantro leaves
12. Your dish is ready to be served.

## 3.12 Udon Soup Recipe

**Preparation Time:** 30 minutes
**Cooking Time:** 20 minutes
**Serving:** 4

**Ingredients:**

- One cup of rice noodles
- One teaspoon of miso paste
- One cup of onion
- One cup of water
- Two tablespoons of minced garlic
- Two tablespoons of minced ginger
- Half cup of cilantro
- One cup of diced carrots
- Two cups of vegetables
- Two tablespoons of olive oil
- One cup of vegetable stock
- One cup of chopped tomatoes

**Instructions:**
1. Take a pan.
2. Add in the oil and onions.

3. Cook the onions until they become soft and fragrant.
4. Add in the chopped garlic and ginger.
5. Cook the mixture and add the tomatoes into it.
6. Add the spices.
7. Add the rice noodles and miso paste into it.
8. Mix the ingredients carefully and cover the pan.
9. Add the vegetables and the rest of the ingredients.
10. Add the water into the mixture and let the mixture boil.
11. Let the soup cook for ten to fifteen minutes straight.
12. Add cilantro on top.
13. Your dish is ready to be served.

## 3.13 Spicy Tofu Katsu Recipe

**Preparation Time:** 30 minutes
**Cooking Time:** 10 minutes
**Serving:** 4

**Ingredients:**

- One teaspoon of bonito powder
- Half cup of cilantro
- Two tablespoons of sesame oil
- One cup of chopped tomatoes
- One cup of lemon juice
- Salt to taste
- Black pepper to taste
- One cup of onion
- One cup of vegetable broth
- One teaspoon of cornstarch
- One cup of panko crumbs
- Two cups of tofu cubes
- Two tablespoons of minced garlic
- Two tablespoons of minced ginger

**Instructions:**
1. Take a pan.
2. Add in the oil and onions.
3. Cook the onions until they become soft and fragrant.
4. Add in the chopped garlic and ginger.
5. Cook the mixture and add the tomatoes into it.
6. Add the spices.
7. Add in the broth and the rest of the curry ingredients.
8. Take a small bowl.
9. Add the panko crumbs and cornstarch.
10. Add all the tofu cubes in the cornstarch mixture.
11. Deep fry the tofu until the curry is getting ready.
12. Dish out the tofu and add it in the curry mixture.
13. Coat the vegetables well.
14. Garnish the dish with chopped cilantro leaves
15. Your dish is ready to be served.

## 3.14 Vegetable Teppanyaki Recipe

**Preparation Time:** 30 minutes
**Cooking Time:** 10 minutes
**Serving:** 4

**Ingredients:**

- Half cup of cilantro
- Two tablespoons of sesame oil
- One cup of chopped tomatoes
- One cup of lemon juice
- One tablespoon of powdered cumin
- Salt to taste
- Black pepper to taste
- One teaspoon of chili paste
- One cup of onion
- Two cups of vegetable pieces
- Two tablespoons of minced garlic
- Two tablespoons of minced ginger

**Instructions:**
1. Take a teppan.
2. Add in the oil and onions.

3. Cook the onions until they become soft and fragrant.
4. Add in the chopped garlic and ginger.
5. Cook the mixture and add the tomatoes into it.
6. Add the spices.
7. Add the vegetable pieces into it.
8. Cook for five minutes.
9. Garnish the dish with chopped cilantro leaves
10.     Your dish is ready to be served.

## 3.15 Vegetarian Okonomiyaki Recipe

**Preparation Time:** 10 minutes
**Cooking Time:** 30 minutes
**Serving:** 4

**Ingredients:**

- Two eggs
- One tablespoon of sliced cabbage
- One tablespoon of maple syrup
- Half cup of coconut milk
- Half cup of white sugar
- A pinch of salt
- One tablespoon of vanilla extract
- Two cups of cake flour
- One cup of butter

**Instructions:**
1. Take a medium bowl and add the eggs, sliced cabbage, and cake flour.
2. Add one cup coconut milk and mix well.
3. Add the sugar, the salt, and the beaten eggs.
4. Mix them well.

5. Add the baking soda in the mixture.
6. Add the maple syrup into it.
7. Mix it for few minutes.
8. Bake the cake for twenty to twenty-five minutes.
9. Your dish is ready to be served.

## 3.16 Vegetarian Sukiyaki Recipe

**Preparation Time:** 20 minutes
**Cooking Time:** 20 minutes
**Serving:** 4

**Ingredients:**

- One tablespoon of oyster sauce
- One cup of rice noodles
- One tablespoon of fish sauce
- Half tablespoon of soy sauce
- Two teaspoons of minced garlic
- Three tablespoons of cooking oil
- Half cup of hot sauce
- Two cups of mixed vegetables
- Salt as needed
- Chopped fresh cilantro for garnishing

**Instructions:**
1. Take a large pan.
2. Add the cooking oil into the pan and heat it.
3. Add the vegetables into the pan and stir-fry it.
4. Add the minced garlic into the pan.

5. Add the soy sauce, fish sauce, noodles, hot sauce, and rest of the ingredients into the mixture.
6. Cook the dish for ten minutes and add some water for curry.
7. Dish out the vegetables and garnish them with chopped fresh cilantro leaves.
8. Your dish is ready to be served.

## 3.17 Spicy Corn Soup Recipe

**Preparation Time:** 30 minutes
**Cooking Time:** 20 minutes
**Serving:** 4

**Ingredients:**

- One cup of corn
- One teaspoon of miso paste
- One cup of onion
- One cup of water
- Two tablespoons of minced garlic
- Two tablespoons of minced ginger
- Half cup of cilantro
- Two tablespoons of chili paste
- Two tablespoons of olive oil
- One cup of vegetable stock
- One cup of chopped tomatoes

**Instructions:**
1. Take a pan.
2. Add in the oil and onions.

3. Cook the onions until they become soft and fragrant.
4. Add in the chopped garlic and ginger.
5. Cook the mixture and add the tomatoes into it.
6. Add the spices.
7. Add the corn and miso paste into it.
8. Mix the ingredients carefully and cover the pan.
9. Add the rest of the ingredients.
10. Add the water into the mixture and let the mixture boil.
11. Let the soup cook for ten to fifteen minutes straight.
12. Add cilantro on top.
13. Your dish is ready to be served.

## 3.18 Teriyaki Mushroom Skewers Recipe

**Preparation Time:** 15 minutes
**Cooking Time:** 20 minutes
**Serving:** 4

**Ingredients:**

- Half pound of whole mushrooms
- Three tablespoons of oil
- Three garlic cloves
- Two tablespoons of ginger
- One cup of teriyaki sauce
- Two teaspoons of salt
- Wooden skewers

**Instructions:**
1. Take a bowl.
2. Add all the ingredients into the bowl.
3. Mix everything well.
4. Add the mushrooms into wooden skewers.
5. Cook the skewers well on all sides.
6. The dish is ready to be served.

## 3.19 Vegetarian Gyoza Recipe

**Preparation Time:** 10 minutes
**Cooking Time:** 30 minutes
**Serving:** 4

**Ingredients:**

- Four flatbreads
- Half cup of vegetable broth
- A quarter cup of lemon juice
- One cup of sweet dipping sauce
- Half cup of sliced red onion
- Half cup of sliced tomatoes
- One tablespoon of minced garlic
- One cup of tomato paste
- Two tablespoons of sesame oil
- One tablespoon of garlic powder
- One tablespoon of soy sauce
- Half teaspoon of ground cinnamon
- Two tablespoons of chili powder
- A pinch of sea salt
- Two cups of mixed vegetables

**Instructions:**

1. Take a large pan.
2. Add the sesame oil and garlic into the pan.
3. Add the tomato paste, smoked paprika, chili powder, soy sauce, and salt.
4. Add the vegetable broth, lemon juice, and vegetables into the pan.
5. Cook the ingredients well for about fifteen minutes.
6. Bake the flatbreads for about two to three minutes.
7. Cut the flatbreads in between to form a pouch structure.
8. Add the cooked mixture into the flatbread and line it with sweet dipping sauce, sliced tomatoes, and red onions.
9. Your dish is ready to be served.

## 3.20 Japanese Kale Soup Recipe

**Preparation Time:** 30 minutes
**Cooking Time:** 20 minutes
**Serving:** 4

**Ingredients:**

- One cup of kale
- One teaspoon of miso paste
- One cup of onion
- One cup of bell peppers
- One cup of water
- Two tablespoons of minced garlic
- Two tablespoons of minced ginger
- Half cup of cilantro
- Two tablespoons of olive oil
- One cup of vegetable stock
- One cup of chopped tomatoes

**Instructions:**
1. Take a pan.
2. Add in the oil and onions.

3. Cook the onions until they become soft and fragrant.
4. Add in the chopped garlic and ginger.
5. Cook the mixture and add the tomatoes into it.
6. Add the spices.
7. Add the kale and miso paste into it.
8. Mix the ingredients carefully and cover the pan.
9. Add the vegetables and the rest of the ingredients.
10. Add the water into the mixture and let the mixture boil.
11. Let the soup cook for ten to fifteen minutes straight.
12. Add cilantro on top.
13. Your dish is ready to be served.

# Chapter 4: Vegetarian Indian Recipes

Indians are known to have a wide variety of vegetarian dishes. Following are some yummy vegetarian recipes that are rich in healthy nutrients:

## 4.1 Roasted Zucchini in Curry Oatmeal Recipe

**Preparation Time:** 10 minutes
**Cooking Time:** 30 minutes
**Serving:** 2

**Ingredients:**

- Half pound of roasted zucchini pieces
- Half pound of oats
- Two onions
- Two tablespoons of canola oil
- Two cups of water
- One teaspoon of ginger
- Two tomatoes
- Four garlic cloves
- Three green chilies
- Salt to taste
- Black pepper to taste

- One teaspoon of coriander leaves
- Half teaspoon of garam masala
- One teaspoon of black mustard seeds
- One teaspoon of cumin seeds

**Instructions:**
1. Take a pan and add the oil in it.
2. Heat the oil and add onions in it.
3. Fry the onions until they become light brown.
4. Add the cumin seeds and mustard seeds in the pan.
5. Fry them well and add salt and pepper and green chilies.
6. Add the turmeric, ginger and garlic cloves in it.
7. Add the zucchini pieces into the pan.
8. Mix them well and continue cooking.
9. Add some water if needed.
10. Add the oats into the cooking mixture.
11. Add the coriander leaves and garam masala as needed.
12. Mix all the ingredients and cook for few minutes.
13. Add the water according to the quantity of curry you want.
14. Your dish is ready to be served.

## 4.2 Spicy Banana Curry Recipe

**Preparation Time:** 10 minutes
**Cooking Time:** 30 minutes
**Serving:** 2

**Ingredients:**

- Half pound of banana pieces
- Two onions
- Two tablespoons of canola oil
- Two cups of water
- One teaspoon of ginger
- Two tomatoes
- Four garlic cloves
- Six green chilies
- Salt to taste
- Black pepper to taste
- One teaspoon of coriander leaves
- Half teaspoon of garam masala
- One teaspoon of black mustard seeds
- One teaspoon of cumin seeds

**Instructions:**
1. Take a pan and add the oil in it.

2. Heat the oil and add onions in it.
3. Fry the onions until they become light brown.
4. Add the cumin seeds and mustard seeds in the pan.
5. Fry them well and add salt and pepper and green chilies.
6. Add the turmeric, ginger and garlic cloves in it.
7. Add the green mangoes into the pan.
8. Mix them well and continue cooking.
9. Add some water if needed.
10. Add the banana pieces into the cooking mixture.
11. Add the coriander leaves and garam masala as needed.
12. Mix all the ingredients and cook for few minutes.
13. Your dish is ready to be served.

## 4.3 Spiced Tofu Skewers Recipe

**Preparation Time:** 15 minutes
**Cooking Time:** 20 minutes
**Serving:** 4

**Ingredients:**

- Half pound of tofu cubes
- Three tablespoons of oil
- Three garlic cloves
- Two tablespoons of mixed spice
- Two tablespoons of ginger
- One cup of yogurt
- Two teaspoons of salt
- Wooden skewers

**Instructions:**
1. Take a bowl.
2. Add all the ingredients into the bowl.
3. Mix everything well.
4. Add the tofu into wooden skewers.
5. Cook the skewers well on all sides.
6. The dish is ready to be served.

## 4.4 Indian Mushroom Rice Recipe

**Preparation Time:** 10 minutes
**Cooking Time:** 30 minutes
**Serving:** 4

**Ingredients:**

- Two cups of rice
- One cup of mushrooms
- Two tablespoons of olive oil
- Two cups of water
- One teaspoon of ginger
- Two tomatoes
- Four garlic cloves
- Three green chilies
- Salt to taste
- Black pepper to taste
- One teaspoon of coriander leaves
- Half teaspoon garam masala
- One teaspoon of black mustard seeds
- One teaspoon of cumin seeds
- Two onions

**Instructions:**

1. Take a pan and add the oil in it.
2. Heat the oil and add onions in it.
3. Fry the onions until they become light brown.
4. Add the cumin seeds, mushrooms, and mustard seeds in the pan.
5. Fry them well and add salt and pepper and green chilies.
6. Add the turmeric, ginger and garlic cloves in it.
7. Mix them well and continue cooking.
8. Cook all the vegetables until they become tender.
9. Add the coriander leaves and garam masala as needed.
10. Mix all the ingredients and cook for few minutes.
11. Boil the rice in water until they become eatable.
12. Mix and cook all the ingredients for about ten minutes.
13. Your dish is ready to be served.

## 4.5 Spicy Palak Tofu Paneer Recipe

**Preparation Time:** 20 minutes
**Cooking Time:** 40 minutes
**Serving:** 4

### Ingredients:

- Two tablespoons of mixed masala
- One pound of tofu cubes
- Two cups of spinach
- Two tomatoes
- One tablespoon of red chili powder
- Three tablespoons of oil
- Three garlic cloves
- Two tablespoon ginger
- One teaspoon of chopped coriander leaves
- Two teaspoons of sea salt
- One cup of chopped cilantro
- Two tablespoons of chopped onions

### Instructions:
1. Take a skillet and add the oil in it.
2. Heat the oil and add onions in it.

3. Fry the onions until they become light brown in color.
4. Add the red chilies in the skillet.
5. Fry it well and add salt and pepper and green chilies.
6. Add the turmeric, ginger and garlic cloves in it.
7. Mix them well and continue cooking.
8. Add the mixed masala and chopped tomatoes as needed.
9. Mix all the ingredients and cook for few minutes.
10. Add spinach and tofu once the mixture is cooked.
11. Place the lid on top and reduce the heat.
12. Dish out when the ingredients are done.
13. Your dish is ready to be served.

## 4.6 Vegetarian Korma Recipe

**Preparation Time:** 10 minutes
**Cooking Time:** 20 minutes
**Serving:** 2

**Ingredients:**

- One pound of mixed vegetables
- One tablespoon of cumin seeds
- Two onions
- Two tablespoons of canola oil
- Two cups of tomato puree
- One teaspoon of ginger
- Four garlic cloves
- Three green chilies
- Salt to taste
- Black pepper to taste
- One teaspoon of coriander leaves
- Half teaspoon of garam masala
- One teaspoon of black mustard seeds
- One teaspoon of Indian black salt

**Instructions:**
1. Take a pan and add the oil in it.
2. Heat the oil and add onions in it.
3. Fry the onions until they become light brown.
4. Add the cumin seeds and mustard seeds in the pan.
5. Fry them well and add salt and pepper and green chilies.
6. Add the turmeric, ginger and garlic cloves in it.
7. Mix them well and continue cooking.
8. Add some tomato puree.
9. Add the vegetables into the cooking mixture.
10. Add the coriander leaves and garam masala as needed.
11. Mix all the ingredients and cook for few minutes.
12. Add the Indian black salt for taste.
13. Your dish is ready to be served.

## 4.7 Indian Cauliflower and Pea Curry Recipe

**Preparation Time:** 10 minutes
**Cooking Time:** 60 minutes
**Serving:** 2

**Ingredients:**

- Half pound of cauliflower
- Half pound of pea
- Two onions
- Two tablespoons of canola oil
- Two cups of water
- One teaspoon of ginger
- Two tomatoes
- Four garlic cloves
- Three green chilies
- Salt to taste
- Black pepper to taste
- One teaspoon of coriander leaves
- Half teaspoon of garam masala
- One teaspoon of black mustard seeds
- One teaspoon of cumin seeds

**Instructions:**

1. Take a pan and add the oil in it.
2. Heat the oil and add onions in it.
3. Fry the onions until they become light brown.
4. Add the cumin seeds and mustard seeds in the pan.
5. Fry them well and add salt and pepper and green chilies.
6. Add the turmeric, ginger and garlic cloves in it.
7. Mix them well and continue cooking.
8. Add some water if needed.
9. Reduce the stove heat.
10. Add the cauliflower and pea into the cooking mixture.
11. Place a lid on top
12. Add the coriander leaves and garam masala as needed.
13. Mix all the ingredients and cook for few minutes.
14. Your dish is ready to be served.

## 4.8 Spicy Chickpea and Mushroom Curry Recipe

**Preparation Time:** 10 minutes
**Cooking Time:** 60 minutes
**Serving:** 2

**Ingredients:**

- Half pound of chickpeas
- Half pound of mushroom
- Two onions
- Two tablespoons of canola oil
- Two cups of water
- One teaspoon of ginger
- Two tomatoes
- Four garlic cloves
- Six green chilies
- Salt to taste
- Black pepper to taste
- One teaspoon of coriander leaves
- Half teaspoon of garam masala
- One teaspoon of black mustard seeds
- One teaspoon of cumin seeds

**Instructions:**
1. Take a pan and add the oil in it.
2. Heat the oil and add onions in it.
3. Fry the onions until they become light brown.
4. Add the cumin seeds and mustard seeds to the pan.
5. Fry them well and add salt and pepper and green chilies.
6. Add the turmeric, ginger and garlic cloves in it.
7. Mix them well and continue cooking.
8. Add some water if needed.
9. Reduce the stove heat.
10. Add the chickpeas and mushrooms into the cooking mixture.
11. Place a lid on top
12. Add the coriander leaves and garam masala as needed.
13. Mix all the ingredients and cook for few minutes.
14. Your dish is ready to be served.

## 4.9 Spicy Pav Bhaji Recipe

**Preparation Time:** 10 minutes
**Cooking Time:** 25 minutes
**Serving:** 2

**Ingredients:**

- Two tablespoons of coconut oil
- One cup of chickpeas
- One onion
- Three garlic cloves
- Two tablespoon ginger
- One teaspoon of cumin seeds
- One teaspoon of chopped coriander leaves
- One teaspoon of cayenne powder
- Two teaspoons of sea salt
- One cup of chopped cilantro
- One tomato
- One pack of bread buns

**Instructions:**
1. Take a skillet and add the coconut oil in it.

2. Heat the oil and add onions in it.
3. Fry the onions until they become light brown in color.
4. Add the cumin seeds and chickpeas in the skillet.
5. Fry them well and add salt and pepper and green chilies.
6. Add the turmeric, ginger and garlic cloves in it.
7. Mix them well and continue cooking.
8. Add some water if needed.
9. Add the coriander leaves and chopped tomatoes as needed.
10. Mix all the ingredients and cook for few minutes.
11. Add chopped cilantro and cayenne powder to taste.
12. Serve the dish with bread buns
13. Your dish is ready to be served.

## 4.10 Indian Roasted Brussel Sprouts Recipe

**Preparation Time:** 15 minutes
**Cooking Time:** 20 minutes
**Serving:** 4

**Ingredients:**

- Half pound of Brussel sprouts
- Three tablespoons of oil
- Three garlic cloves
- Two tablespoons of mixed spice
- Two tablespoons of ginger
- One cup of yogurt
- Two teaspoons of salt

**Instructions:**
1. Take a bowl.
2. Add all the ingredients into the bowl.
3. Mix everything well.
4. Add the Brussel sprouts into a baking tray.
5. Bake the Brussel sprouts well.
6. The dish is ready to be served.

## 4.11 Indian Sultani Daal Recipe

**Preparation Time:** 10 minutes
**Cooking Time:** 60 minutes
**Serving:** 2

**Ingredients:**

- Half pound of red lentils
- Two onions
- Two tablespoons of butter
- Two cups of water
- One teaspoon of ginger
- Two tomatoes
- Four garlic cloves
- Three green chilies
- Salt to taste
- Black pepper to taste
- One teaspoon of coriander leaves
- Half teaspoon of garam masala
- One teaspoon of black mustard seeds
- One teaspoon of cumin seeds

**Instructions:**
1. Take a pan and add the butter in it.
2. Heat the oil and add onions in it.
3. Fry the onions until they become light brown in color.
4. Add the cumin seeds and mustard seeds in the pan.
5. Fry them well and add salt and pepper and green chilies.
6. Add the turmeric, ginger and garlic cloves in it.
7. Mix them well and continue cooking.
8. Add some water if needed.
9. Reduce the stove heat.
10. Add the lentils into the cooking mixture.
11. Place a lid on top
12. After twenty minutes, add the coriander leaves and garam masala as needed.
13. Mix all the ingredients and cook for few minutes.
14. Your dish is ready to be served.

## 4.12 Indian Curried Okra and Eggplant with Chickpea Recipe

**Preparation Time:** 10 minutes
**Cooking Time:** 60 minutes
**Serving:** 2

**Ingredients:**

- Half pound of chickpeas
- Half pound of okra
- Two cups of eggplant
- Two onions
- Two tablespoons of canola oil
- Two cups of water
- One teaspoon of ginger
- Two tomatoes
- Four garlic cloves
- Three green chilies
- Salt to taste
- Black pepper to taste
- One teaspoon of coriander leaves
- Half teaspoon of garam masala
- One teaspoon of black mustard seeds

- One teaspoon of cumin seeds

## Instructions:

1. Take a pan and add the oil in it.
2. Heat the oil and add onions in it.
3. Fry the onions until they become light brown in color.
4. Add the cumin seeds and mustard seeds in the pan.
5. Fry them well and add salt and pepper and green chilies.
6. Add the chickpeas, turmeric, ginger and garlic cloves in it.
7. Mix them well and continue cooking.
8. Add some water if needed.
9. Reduce the stove heat.
10. Add the okra and eggplant into the cooking mixture.
11. Place a lid on top
12. After twenty minutes, add the coriander leaves and garam masala as needed.
13. Mix all the ingredients and cook for few minutes.
14. Your dish is ready to be served.

## 4.13 Creamy Halloumi Recipe

**Preparation Time:** 10 minutes
**Cooking Time:** 60 minutes
**Serving:** 2

**Ingredients:**

- Half pound of halloumi pieces
- Half cup of cream
- Two onions
- Two tablespoons of canola oil
- Two cups of water
- One teaspoon of ginger
- Two tomatoes
- Four garlic cloves
- Three green chilies
- Salt to taste
- Black pepper to taste
- One teaspoon of coriander leaves
- Half teaspoon of garam masala
- One teaspoon of black mustard seeds
- One teaspoon of cumin seeds

**Instructions:**
1. Take a pan and add the oil in it.
2. Heat the oil and add onions in it.
3. Fry the onions until they become light brown in color.
4. Add the cumin seeds and mustard seeds in the pan.
5. Fry them well and add salt and pepper and green chilies.
6. Add the turmeric, ginger and garlic cloves in it.
7. Mix them well and continue cooking.
8. Add some water if needed.
9. Reduce the stove heat.
10. Add the halloumi pieces into the cooking mixture.
11. Place a lid on top
12. Add the coriander leaves and garam masala as needed.
13. Mix all the ingredients and cook for few minutes.
14. Add the cream and mix well.
15. Cook the dish for five minutes.
16. Your dish is ready to be served.

## 4.14 Indian Bottle Gourd Dal Recipe

**Preparation Time:** 10 minutes
**Cooking Time:** 60 minutes
**Serving:** 2

**Ingredients:**

- Half pound of bottle gourd
- Half pound of parboiled lentils
- Two onions
- Two tablespoons of canola oil
- Two cups of water
- One teaspoon of ginger
- Two tomatoes
- Four garlic cloves
- Three green chilies
- Salt to taste
- Black pepper to taste
- One teaspoon of coriander leaves
- Half teaspoon of garam masala
- One teaspoon of black mustard seeds
- One teaspoon of cumin seeds

**Instructions:**

1. Take a pan and add the oil in it.
2. Heat the oil and add onions in it.
3. Fry the onions until they become light brown in color.
4. Add the cumin seeds and mustard seeds in the pan.
5. Fry them well and add salt and pepper and green chilies.
6. Add the turmeric, ginger and garlic cloves in it.
7. Mix them well and continue cooking.
8. Add some water if needed.
9. Reduce the stove heat.
10. Add the parboiled lentils and bottle gourd into the cooking mixture.
11. Place a lid on top
12. Add the coriander leaves and garam masala as needed.
13. Mix all the ingredients and cook for few minutes.
14. Your dish is ready to be served.

## 4.15 Indian Cabbage Palya Recipe

**Preparation Time:** 10 minutes
**Cooking Time:** 60 minutes
**Serving:** 2

**Ingredients:**

- Half pound of cabbage
- Two onions
- Two tablespoons of canola oil
- Two cups of water
- One teaspoon of ginger
- Four garlic cloves
- Three green chilies
- Salt to taste
- Black pepper to taste
- One teaspoon of coriander leaves
- Half teaspoon of garam masala
- One teaspoon of black mustard seeds
- One teaspoon of cumin seeds

**Instructions:**
1. Take a pan and add the oil in it.

2. Heat the oil and add onions in it.
3. Fry the onions until they become light brown in color.
4. Add the cumin seeds and mustard seeds in the pan.
5. Fry them well and add salt and pepper and green chilies.
6. Add the turmeric, ginger and garlic cloves in it.
7. Mix them well and continue cooking.
8. Add the cabbage into the cooking mixture.
9. Add the coriander leaves and garam masala.
10. Mix all the ingredients and cook for few minutes.
11. Your dish is ready to be served.

## 4.16 Spicy Kale and Potato Curry Recipe

**Preparation Time:** 10 minutes
**Cooking Time:** 60 minutes
**Serving:** 2

**Ingredients:**

- Half pound of kale
- Half pound of potato
- Two onions
- Two tablespoons of canola oil
- Two cups of water
- One teaspoon of ginger
- Two tomatoes
- Four garlic cloves
- Six green chilies
- Salt to taste
- Black pepper to taste
- One teaspoon of coriander leaves
- Half teaspoon of garam masala
- One teaspoon of black mustard seeds
- One teaspoon of cumin seeds

**Instructions:**
1. Take a pan and add the oil in it.
2. Heat the oil and add onions in it.
3. Fry the onions until they become light brown in color.
4. Add the cumin seeds and mustard seeds in the pan.
5. Fry them well and add salt and pepper and green chilies.
6. Add the turmeric, ginger and garlic cloves in it.
7. Mix them well and continue cooking.
8. Add some water if needed.
9. Reduce the stove heat.
10. Add the kale and potato into the cooking mixture.
11. Place a lid on top
12. Add the coriander leaves and garam masala as needed.
13. Mix all the ingredients and cook for few minutes.
14. Your dish is ready to be served.

## 4.17 Indian Mint Rice Recipe

**Preparation Time:** 10 minutes
**Cooking Time:** 30 minutes
**Serving:** 4

**Ingredients:**

- Two cups of rice
- One cup of mint
- Two tablespoons of olive oil
- Two cups of water
- One teaspoon of ginger
- Two tomatoes
- Four garlic cloves
- Three green chilies
- Salt to taste
- Black pepper to taste
- One teaspoon of coriander leaves
- Half teaspoon garam masala
- One teaspoon of black mustard seeds
- One teaspoon of cumin seeds
- Two onions

**Instructions:**
1. Take a pan and add the oil in it.
2. Heat the oil and add onions in it.
3. Fry the onions until they become light brown in color.
4. Add the cumin seeds, mint, and mustard seeds in the pan.
5. Fry them well and add salt and pepper and green chilies.
6. Add the turmeric, ginger and garlic cloves in it.
7. Mix them well and continue cooking.
8. Add the coriander leaves and garam masala as needed.
9. Mix all the ingredients and cook for few minutes.
10. Boil the rice in water until they become eatable.
11. Mix and cook all the ingredients for about ten minutes.
12. Your dish is ready to be served.

## 4.18 Indian Garlic Butter Naan Bread Recipe

**Preparation Time:** 30 minutes
**Cooking Time:** 20 minutes
**Serving:** 4

**Ingredients:**

- One teaspoon of garlic powder
- One cup of unsalted butter
- Two tablespoons of chopped coriander
- Four naans

**Instructions:**
1. Take a bowl.
2. Add the garlic powder, unsalted butter, and coriander into the bowl.
3. Mix well.
4. Spread the mixture on top of the naan and heat well.
5. Your dish is ready to be served.

## 4.19 Indian Mango Curry Recipe

**Preparation Time:** 10 minutes
**Cooking Time:** 30 minutes
**Serving:** 2

**Ingredients:**

- Half pound of mango pieces
- Two onions
- Two tablespoons of canola oil
- Two cups of water
- One teaspoon of ginger
- Two tomatoes
- Four garlic cloves
- Three green chilies
- Salt to taste
- Black pepper to taste
- One teaspoon of coriander leaves
- Half teaspoon of garam masala
- One teaspoon of black mustard seeds
- One teaspoon of cumin seeds

**Instructions:**
1. Take a pan and add the oil in it.
2. Heat the oil and add onions in it.
3. Fry the onions until they become light brown in color.
4. Add the cumin seeds and mustard seeds in the pan.
5. Fry them well and add salt and pepper and green chilies.
6. Add the turmeric, ginger and garlic cloves in it.
7. Add the green mangoes into the pan.
8. Mix them well and continue cooking.
9. Add some water if needed.
10. Add the coriander leaves and garam masala as needed.
11. Mix all the ingredients and cook for few minutes.
12. Your dish is ready to be served.

## 4.20 Indian Chickpea Pancakes Recipe

**Preparation Time:** 20 minutes
**Cooking Time:** 20 minutes
**Serving:** 4

**Ingredients:**

- Two tablespoons of pure ghee
- Two tablespoons of condensed milk
- One and a half cups of chickpea flour
- Two eggs
- Half cup of water

**Instructions:**
1. Take a large pan.
2. Add the pure ghee into it.
3. Add the rest of the ingredients into a bowl.
4. Spread the pancake mixture in the ghee.
5. Cook the on both sides until it turns golden brown.
6. The dish is ready to be served.

# Conclusion

Every country in Asia has its fundamental dishes and culinary styles. However, preparing Asian food at home does not mean having difficulty in cooking. Health and taste are always a top priority in Asia, so all the recipes that originated from this continent are extremely healthy and delicious.

This cookbook makes it easy for you to prepare your favorite Asian recipes inside your kitchen without any stress. This cookbook incorporates 80 healthy plans that contain Thai recipes, Indian recipes, Chinese recipes, and Japanese that you can undoubtedly make at home very easily. So, start cooking today with this wonderful cookbook!

# VEGETARIAN WOK
# COOKBOOK

*70 Easy Recipes For Traditional Asian Food*

---

**Maki Blanc**

© **Copyright 2021 by (Maki Blanc) - All rights reserved.**

This document is geared towards providing exact and reliable information in regards to the topic and issue covered. The publication is sold with the idea that the publisher is not required to render accounting, officially permitted, or otherwise, qualified services. If advice is necessary, legal or professional, a practiced individual in the profession should be ordered.

- From a Declaration of Principles which was accepted and approved equally by a Committee of the American Bar Association and a Committee of Publishers and Associations.

It is not legal in any way to reproduce, duplicate, or transmit any part of this document in either electronic means or in printed format. Recording of this publication is strictly prohibited and any storage of this document is not allowed unless with written permission from the publisher. All rights reserved.

The information provided herein is stated to be truthful and consistent, in that any liability, in terms of inattention or otherwise, by any usage or abuse of any policies, processes, or directions contained within is the solitary and utter responsibility of the recipient reader. Under no circumstances will any legal responsibility or blame be held against the publisher for any reparation, damages, or monetary loss due to the information herein, either directly or indirectly.

Respective authors own all copyrights not held by the publisher.

The information herein is offered for informational purposes solely, and is universal as so. The presentation of the information is without contract or any type of guarantee assurance.

The trademarks that are used are without any consent, and the publication of the trademark is without permission or backing by the trademark owner. All trademarks and brands within this book are for clarifying purposes only and are the owned by the owners themselves, not affiliated with this document.

# Contents

**INTRODUCTION** .................................................. 172

**CHAPTER 1: VEGETARIAN WOK INDIAN RECIPES**
................................................................... 174

1.1 Indian Five-Spice Vegetable Stir-Fry ............................. 174

1.2 Wok-Seared Vegetables ......................................... 175

1.3 Noodles and Vegetables Stir Fry ................................ 176

1.4 Indian Stir-Fried Carrots ...................................... 177

1.5 Vegetables in Hot Garlic Sauce ................................. 178

1.6 Stir-Fried Exotic Oriental Vegetable Recipe .................... 179

1.7 Potato and Green Beans Stir Fry ................................ 180

1.8 Balti Stir-Fried Vegetables with Cashews ....................... 181

1.9 Stir-Fried Indian Okra with Spices ............................. 182

1.10 Vegetable Jalfrezi ........................................... 183

1.11 Quinoa Fried Rice Recipe ..................................... 184

1.12 Chili Paneer ................................................ 186

1.13 Frozen Mixed Vegetable Fry ................................... 187

1.14 Curry Fried Rice ............................................ 188

1.15 South Indian Brinjal Stir Fry ................................ 189

1.16 Indian-Spiced Pickled Vegetables ............................. 190

1.17 Cashew Chickpea Curry ....................................... 192

1.18 Stir-Fried Chili Greens .................................................... 193

## CHAPTER 2: VEGETARIAN WOK JAPANESE RECIPES ............................................................................... 195

2.1 Yasai Itame.................................................................. 195

2.2 Japanese Stir-Fried Noodles with Veggies ...................... 196

2.3 Lightly Fried Japanese Vegetables ................................. 197

2.4 Vegan Stir-Fried Udon Noodles....................................... 198

2.5 Vegetable Yakisoba ....................................................... 199

2.6 Hibachi Vegetables........................................................ 200

2.7 Wagamama Wok-Fried Greens ...................................... 200

2.8 Vegan Mapo Nasu.......................................................... 201

2.9 15 Minute Spicy Udon Stir Fry....................................... 202

2.10 Stir-Fried Tofu with Vegetables.................................... 203

2.11 Japanese Mushroom Stir-Fry ....................................... 205

2.12 Veggie Stir-Fry Soba Noodle ........................................ 206

2.13 Speedy Japanese Miso Stir Fry & Sticky Rice .............. 208

2.14 Japanese Shrimp & Eggplant Fried Rice...................... 210

2.15 Vegan Ramen............................................................... 210

2.16 Vegetable Lo Mein........................................................ 212

2.17 Szechuan Eggplant ...................................................... 213

## CHAPTER 3: VEGETARIAN WOK CHINESE RECIPES ............................................................................... 215

3.1 Saucy Vegetable Stir Fry................................................ 215

3.2 Vegetable Stir-Fry Noodles ................................................. 216

3.3 Ginger Veggie Stir Fry ...................................................... 217

3.4 Stir-Fried Lettuce with Garlic Chiles ................................. 218

3.5 Wok Black Bean Glaze and Tossed Veggies in Honey Recipe ................................................................................................. 218

3.6 Shrimp and Chinese Vegetable Stir-Fry ......................... 219

3.7 Black Bean Sauce with Stir Fry Veggies ......................... 220

3.8 Spring Veggie Stir-Fry ..................................................... 221

3.9 Chinese Cabbage Stir-Fry ............................................... 222

3.10 Veggie and Tofu Stir-Fry ............................................... 224

3.11 Seitan Stir-Fry and Vegan Chinese Vegetable Recipe .... 225

3.12 Tofu Stir-Fry with Garlic Sauce ................................... 226

3.13 Chinese Broccoli with Oyster Sauce ............................ 227

3.14 Ramen Stir Fry .............................................................. 228

3.15 Chinese Fried Rice ....................................................... 230

3.16 Cashew Stir Fry Kale Mushroom ................................ 231

3.17 Vegetables in Hot Garlic Sauce ................................... 231

3.18 Stir-Fried Chinese Egg Noodles with Oyster Sauce ....... 233

## CHAPTER 4: VEGETARIAN WOK THAI RECIPES ..235

4.1 Thai Stir-Fried Vegetables with Garlic, Ginger, and Lime 235

4.2 Thai Stir-Fried Mixed Vegetables Recipe ....................... 237

4.3 Vegetarian Thai Noodles ................................................. 238

4.4 Easy Thai Basil Vegetable Stir Fry ................................. 239

4.5 Spicy Thai Basil Fried Rice ............................................. 240

4.6 Thai Vegetable Fried Rice with Cashews ........................ 242

4.7 Vegetarian Thai Yellow Curry ......................................... 243

4.8 Thai Satay Stir-Fry ......................................................... 244

4.9 Vegetarian Pad See Ew with Tofu and Chinese Eggplant . 245

4.10 Veggie Thai Red Curry ................................................. 246

4.11 Easy Vegetable Stir Fry with Creamy Peanut Sauce ...... 247

4.12 Thai Morning Glory Stir Fry ......................................... 249

4.13 Thai Combination Fried Rice ....................................... 249

4.14 Vegetarian Pad Thai with Zoodles ............................... 250

4.15 Thai Stir-Fry with Coconut Rice .................................. 252

4.16 Thai Green Curry with Homemade Curry Paste ........... 254

4.17 Rainbow Vegetarian Pad Thai with Crispy Noodles ....... 254

## CONCLUSION ..................................................... 256

# Introduction

Wok cooking is a Chinese cooking method in which materials are mixed or flipped in a wok while still frying in a tiny portion of very hot oil. The method began in Asia and recent decades has expanded into other Asian countries and the West.

In a hot skillet or wok, wok cooking is a simple way to cook small food bites. The food is continuously stirred when cooking in a wok, as the name implies. The food is pickled when it comes into contact with the wok, which tends to lock in the flavor. Wok cooking is ideal for a wide range of foods, including meat, fish, and veggies. In contrast to deep-frying, the method uses a lot less oil. This process can be used to prepare a variety of fruits, meats, fish, and poultry.

Wok preparation is not only fast and simple, but it is also nutritious. It produces tender-crisp veggies with more nutrients than steamed veggies. The fat content is poor since wok preparation only uses a limited amount of oil.

In a skillet, which is a bowl-shaped pot, an authentic wok recipe is prepared. For mixing, you'll need a heat-resistant spoon or a big spoon. Choose a high-smoke-point oil for a wok dish since it will be cooked at elevated temperatures. This means the oil would not create any smoke or have an unpleasant odor.

Because wok-cooked foods are not heated as much as deep-fried items, they hold the majority of the nutritional values. As a consequence, this cooking process is much healthier. If you intend on doing a lot of wok preparation, make sure your workspace is well ventilated because this cooking method can produce a lot of smoke. As a result, wok dishes made with vegan products are healthier to consume.

"Vegetarian Wok Cookbook" is a complete recipe book based on all-vegetarian wok dishes from India, Japan, China, and Thailand. It has four chapters with detailed knowledge of vegetarian wok cuisine. Try these dishes at your home and make your meals more like Indians.

# Chapter 1: Vegetarian Wok Indian Recipes

## 1.1 Indian Five-Spice Vegetable Stir-Fry

**Cooking Time:** 30 minutes
**Serving Size:** 2
**Ingredients:**
- 1 teaspoon panch phoran
- Salt and freshly ground black pepper
- 3 tablespoon sriracha chili sauce
- 15g fresh coriander
- 150g asparagus
- 4 garlic cloves
- 100g mange tout
- 1 courgette
- 1 carrot
- 1 red pepper
- 2 spring onions
- 1 large red chili
- 6 tablespoon olive oil

**Method:**
1. In a skillet or a large nonstick deep fryer, heat two tablespoons of the oil over medium temperature.
2. Stir-fry for three minutes with all the veggies except the cloves.
3. Salt and pepper to taste.
4. Toss the veggies with the sriracha and coriander leaves and toss well.
5. Heat the remaining four tablespoons of olive oil in the meantime.
6. Fry the garlic until it turns lightly browned.
7. Warm the garlic with the Indian five-spice powder.

8. Stir in the herb and five-spice combination to coat the veggies.
9. Serve the stir-fry as soon as possible.

## 1.2 Wok-Seared Vegetables

**Cooking Time:** 35 minutes
**Serving Size:** 4
   **Ingredients:**
- 1 tablespoon lime juice
- ½ cup fresh mint leaves
- 4 large cloves of garlic
- 3 dried red chilies
- 2 teaspoons coriander seeds
- 1 large green bell pepper
- 1 small red onion
- 3 tablespoons canola oil
- 2 large carrots
- 1 teaspoon cumin seeds
- ½ teaspoon ground turmeric
- 1 tablespoon cornstarch
- ¾ teaspoon salt
- 1 teaspoon fennel seeds

**Method:**
1. Use a spice slicer or a pestle and mortar to grind cardamom, smoked paprika, and fennel seeds.
2. Add cornflour, salt, and fenugreek to a medium mixing bowl and whisk to blend.
3. Stir in the veggies until they are evenly covered in the spice mixture.
4. Heat a large cast-iron pan or wok with a flat surface over high heat.
5. Add two tablespoon extra virgin olive oil.
6. Carrots, red pepper, cabbage, cloves, and chilies should all be added.

7. Heat, occasionally stirring, for four to eight minutes, or until the veggies begin to fry.
8. Turn down the heat to moderate and drizzle in the remaining one tablespoon of oil.
9. Heat with the ingredients from the dish.
10. Cook, constantly stirring, until the vegetables, lemon zest, and mint are heated through, around thirty seconds.

## 1.3 Noodles and Vegetables Stir Fry

**Cooking Time:** 15 minutes
**Serving Size:** 2
**Ingredients:**
- 2 tablespoon soy sauce
- 1 teaspoon white wine vinegar
- 2 spring onions
- 85g beansprout
- 150g pack egg noodle
- 1 yellow pepper
- 100g mange tout
- 1 tablespoon vegetable oil
- 2 garlic cloves
- 1 large carrot
- 2.5cm ginger

**Method:**
1. In a slow cooker or wide, deep fryer, add the oil, whisk the onion, ginger, cabbage, peppers, mange tout, sugar pick, or green beans for 2-3 minutes over medium temperature.
2. Drain the pasta completely, then stir-fry for two minutes with the vegetables and beansprouts.
3. Combine the sesame oil and vinegar in a mixing bowl, then mix into the skillet and stir for 1-two minutes.

4. Mix thoroughly by dividing between individual plates or cups.

## 1.4 Indian Stir-Fried Carrots

**Cooking Time:** 13 minutes
**Serving Size:** 4
   **Ingredients:**
- ¼ cup coconut
- 2-3 tablespoon cilantro
- ½ teaspoon salt
- ¼ cup water
- 5 medium carrots
- 2 dried red chilies
- 1 teaspoon grated ginger
- 1-2 tablespoon olive oil
- 1 teaspoon urad dal
- 4-5 curry leaves
- 1 teaspoon whole mustard seeds

**Method:**
1. In a deep fryer or skillet, heat the oil until it shimmers, then insert the urad dal.
2. Add bay leaves, coriander powder, and dry bell peppers after about 20 seconds, and cook until the seeds start to pop.
3. Heat for one moment with the cut carrots, spice, and salt before adding the water.
4. Decrease to a low heat environment, cover, and boil until carrots are tender around 20 minutes.
5. Remove the lid, add the grated coconut and coriander, and toss all together.
6. Serve after tasting and adding more salt if necessary.

# 1.5 Vegetables in Hot Garlic Sauce

**Cooking Time:** 20 minutes
**Serving Size:** 4
  **Ingredients:**
  **Other Ingredients**
- 2 tablespoon cornflour
- 4 cup water
- Salt to taste
- ½ teaspoon black pepper
- 4 whole dry red chilies
- 2 tablespoon white vinegar
- 4 tablespoon sesame oil
- 1 tablespoon ginger
- 2 tablespoon celery
- 8 -10 garlic cloves
- 2 tablespoon cooking oil

**Hot Garlic Sauce**
- 1 teaspoon red chili flakes
- ¼ cup red chili sauce
- 1 tablespoon brown sugar
- 2 tablespoon soy sauce

**Vegetables**
- 1 cup baby corn
- 1 cup zucchini
- 1 cup red bell pepper
- 1 cup mushrooms
- 1 cup green capsicum
- 1 cup yellow bell pepper
- 1 large-size onion, diced

**Ingredients for Garnish**
- 1 tablespoon peanuts
- 1 fresh red chili
- 1 tablespoon spring onion greens

**Method:**
1. Mix ½ cup water with cornflour and set aside.
2. Brown sugar, red chili flakes, sesame oil, and spicy mayo should all be combined.
3. In a broiler pan or stir-fry bowl, heat the olive oil.
4. Stir-fry all of the veggies except for the onion.
5. In the same broiler pan, warm sesame oil.
6. Add parsley, whole green chilies, pepper, and fennel, thinly sliced.
7. Stir in the diced onion for about a minute or until the onion is translucent.
8. Put in the white vinegar and thoroughly combine all of the components to glaze the plate.
9. Add the hot garlic sauce mix that has been prepared.
10. Salt and chili flakes to taste.
11. Mix in the stir-fried veggies until the sauce has thickened. Switch the heat on.
12. Add green onions, crushed peanuts, and red chili to the gravy as a garnish.

## 1.6 Stir-Fried Exotic Oriental Vegetable Recipe

**Cooking Time:** 15 minutes
**Serving Size:** 2
**Ingredients:**
- 30 ml veg stock
- 3 ml sesame oil
- 20-gram carrot
- 15 ml oyster sauce
- 30-gram bok choy
- 20-gram asparagus
- 20-gram zucchini
- 30-gram broccoli

- 2-gram sugar
- 30-gram Chinese cabbage
- 20-gram snow peas
- 10 ml virgin olive oil
- 10-gram garlic
- 30-gram mushroom

**Method:**
1. To start the food preparation, add the oil to the skillet and insert the minced garlic.
2. Sauté for a minimum of 30 seconds.
3. In a skillet, add blanched veggies.
4. Add sesame oil, salt, soup powder, starch, and stock after that.
5. Cook for a minute while stirring.
6. Pour sesame oil over the dish to finish it off.
7. Serve immediately on a plate with green onions as a garnish.

## 1.7 Potato and Green Beans Stir Fry

**Cooking Time:** 35 minutes
**Serving Size:** 5
**Ingredients:**
- 250 green beans
- Salt to season
- 1 teaspoon of chili fleck
- 2-3 red chilies
- 3 tablespoons of oil
- ½ teaspoon of turmeric powder
- ¼ cup water
- 2 garlic cloves
- 2 medium-sized potatoes
- 1 medium-sized onion
- A sprig of curry leaves

**Method:**

1. Potatoes should be cut into chunks.
2. Set down the green beans after they have been washed.
3. Position the cooking pan on the stove and add in the oil; wait a few seconds for the oil to heat up.
4. Stir in the curry leaves, tomatoes, and cloves, and cook for a few minutes.
5. To the tempering components, pour the mixture and then the turmeric powder and simmer.
6. ¼ cup water should be poured in.
7. Start to sauté with chili flakes and diced peppers.
8. Add the Brussels sprouts to the boil and sprinkle with salt.
9. Test for spice, add salt if needed, and serve hot once the bean is heated through.

## 1.8 Balti Stir-Fried Vegetables with Cashews

**Cooking Time:** 30 minutes
**Serving Size:** 4
   **Ingredients:**
- Steamed rice
- 50g toasted cashew nuts
- 60 ml vegetable stock
- 75g English spinach leaves
- 300g slender eggplants
- 3 ripe tomatoes
- Two tablespoons vegetable oil
- 70g balti curry paste
- 1 onion

**Method:**
1. Heat a skillet or a deep cooking pot to a high temperature.
2. Swirl in the oil to evenly cover the side.
3. Boil the onions for 3-4 minutes over medium temperature or until translucent.

4. Heat for 1 minute after adding the curry paste, then insert the eggplant and cook over medium heat.
5. Gently throw in the tofu for four minutes or until translucent.
6. Cook for three minutes, or until the tomato is tender, after adding the tomato and stock.
7. Cook, constantly stirring, until the spinach is only wilted.
8. Season with salt and pepper to taste, then serve.

## 1.9 Stir-Fried Indian Okra with Spices

**Cooking Time:** 15 minutes
**Serving Size:** 4
**Ingredients:**
- Salt to taste
- 2 tablespoon cilantro
- 1 teaspoon amchur
- ½ teaspoon garam masala
- 1 pound okra
- ½ teaspoon turmeric
- ½ teaspoon paprika
- 1 tablespoon vegetable oil
- 1 green chili pepper
- 1 tablespoon coriander powder
- 2 cloves garlic
- ½ inch ginger
- 1 medium onion
- 2 medium tomatoes
- 1 teaspoon cumin seeds

**Method:**
1. Position the okra in a steamer basket with ½ teaspoon of oil.

2. For an 8-minute air fried, preheat the oven to 375°F.
3. In a skillet, heat the remaining oil.
4. Transfer the cumin seeds and a bit of salt after they have darkened slightly.
5. Sauté the vegetables until they are transparent and starting to brown.
6. Combine the ginger, cloves, and green hot peppers in a mixing bowl.
7. Mix in the tomatoes, then insert the seasoning.
8. Put a cup of water to a boil with the onions and tomatoes.
9. Sprinkle with salt and transfer the okra that has been prepared to the sauce.
10. Serve immediately with a garnish of cilantro.

## 1.10 Vegetable Jalfrezi

**Cooking Time:** 15 minutes
**Serving Size:** 4
**Ingredients:**
- Few mint leaves
- 3 tablespoon oil divided
- 1 teaspoon garam masala
- 1 tablespoon white vinegar
- ¾ cup bell peppers
- 2 tablespoon red chili powder
- Salt to taste
- ½ cup carrots and string beans
- 1 teaspoon cumin seeds
- 1 teaspoon onion seeds
- ½ cup cauliflower florets
- 1 cup diced tomatoes
- Few shreds of ginger

- ½ cup paneer
- ¾ cup onions

**Method:**
1. Heat the vegetables, green beans, and florets for five minutes in hot water.
2. In a skillet, heat ½ teaspoon oil.
3. Sauté the paneer pieces until golden brown.
4. In the same bowl, add around ½ teaspoon oil and the vegetables and bell peppers.
5. In the same pan, make two tablespoons of oil.
6. Insert the cumin and onion seeds when the pan is heated.
7. Cook until the tomatoes are mushy and the oil extracts, then add the diced tomatoes.
8. Combine the paprika, curry powder, and salt in a cup.
9. Combine the onion-pepper mixture and the sautéed veggies in a large mixing bowl.
10. Combine the ground ginger and the vinegar in a mixing bowl. Combine all of the ingredients, including the paneer that has been sautéed.
11. Heat to a high temperature. Serve with the mint leaves.

## 1.11 Quinoa Fried Rice Recipe

**Cooking Time:** 30 minutes
**Serving Size:** 4
**Ingredients:**
- 3 large eggs
- Thinly sliced green onions
- 2 cloves garlic
- 2 tablespoon soy sauce
- 1 cup quinoa
- 1 large carrot
- 1 ½ cup frozen peas

- 1 tablespoon. sesame oil
- 1 large onion
- Kosher salt

**Method:**
1. Take 2 cups of water and brown rice to a boil in a small saucepan.
2. Cover and simmer for 20 minutes, or until all of the water has been absorbed.
3. Fluff with a fork after seasoning with salt.
4. Add the oil to a large frying pan.
5. Cook, occasionally stirring, until the onion, carrot, and peas are tender around 10 to 15 minutes.
6. Cook for another minute until the garlic and soy sauces are fragrant.
7. Scramble the eggs for 1 to 2 minutes.
8. Three minutes after adding the cooked quinoa, heat completely.
9. Cover with spring onions and rain of sesame oil.

## 1.12 Chili Paneer

**Cooking Time:** 30 minutes
**Serving Size:** 3
### Ingredients:
### For Paneer Pakoda
- 9 cubes paneer
- Oil for deep frying
- ½ teaspoon ginger-garlic paste
- ¼ cup water
- 1 teaspoon soy sauce
- ¼ teaspoon salt
- ¼ cup cornflour
- ½ teaspoon pepper
- ½ teaspoon red chili powder
- ¼ cup all-purpose flour

### For Gravy
- 1 tablespoon cornflour
- 1 cup water
- ¼ teaspoon pepper
- ¼ teaspoon salt
- 4 teaspoon oil
- 2 tablespoon soy sauce
- 1 tablespoon chili sauce
- ½ capsicum
- 2 tablespoon vinegar
- 2 cloves garlic
- 2 tablespoon onion
- 2 green chili
- 4 tablespoon spring onion

**Method:**
1. To begin, make a corn flour batter with seasoning.

2. Paneer pieces are then dipped in egg and deep-fried in hot oil.
3. Fry the paneer until golden brown and crispy.
4. Heat 4 teaspoon oil and sauté cloves to make the gravy.
5. Spring tomato, onion, and green chili are also good additions.
6. In addition, insert ½ capsicum and gently sauté.
7. Add vinegar, sesame oil, chili sauce, pepper, and salt to taste.
8. Cook over high heat until the mixture thickens.
9. Pour in the cornflour water and keep stirring.
10. Add the paneer that has been fried.
11. Finally, prepare the fried rice with the chili paneer gravy.

## 1.13 Frozen Mixed Vegetable Fry

**Cooking Time:** 10 minutes
**Serving Size:** 6
  **Ingredients:**
- 1 package frozen vegetables
- 2 tablespoons soy sauce
- 2 teaspoons peanut butter
- 1 tablespoon brown sugar
- 2 teaspoons garlic powder
- 2 teaspoons olive oil

**Method:**
1. In a shallow saucepan, mix soy sauce, garlic powder, red pepper, and cottage cheese.
2. In a medium saucepan, heat the oil over moderate heat and cook and stir the fresh veggies until they are just tender around 6 to 10 minutes.
3. Remove the pan from the heat and stir in the soy sauce combination.

## 1.14 Curry Fried Rice

**Cooking Time:** 30 minutes
**Serving Size:** 4
### Ingredients:
- ¼ cup scallions
- Freshly parsley
- ½ cup frozen corn
- Kosher salt and black pepper
- 2 tablespoon Tamari
- ½ cup frozen peas
- 2 eggs
- 1.5 tablespoon curry powder
- 1 large carrot
- 1 cup mushrooms
- 4 cups cooked rice
- 1 yellow onion
- 1 rib of celery
- 3 garlic cloves
- 2 tablespoon olive oil

**Method:**
1. In a medium saucepan or skillet, heat the oil over medium heat.
2. Simmer with the onions and garlic.
3. Combine the celery, broccoli, and herbs in a large mixing bowl.
4. Add the garam masala, kosher salt, and salt and pepper to taste.
5. Wipe the veggies to the bottom of the plate; if necessary, add a little more oil. In the middle of the plate, pour the egg mixture.
6. In quantities, add the rice to the pan and whisk to coat.
7. Mix in the tamari or soy sauce thoroughly.

8. Insert the green onion, green beans, and canned corn at the top.
9. Reduce the heat to low and gently press the rice into a bowl.
10. If required, season with salt and black pepper.
11. Serve immediately after removing the skillet from the heat and garnishing it with freshly grated parmesan.

## 1.15 South Indian Brinjal Stir Fry

**Cooking Time:** 35 minutes
**Serving Size:** 4
   **Ingredients:**
- 2 teaspoons salt
- 1–2 teaspoons red chili powder
- 1 teaspoon urad dal
- 1 teaspoon asafetida powder
- 5 tablespoon vegetable oil
- 1 teaspoon mustard seeds
- 1 onion
- 8–10 ripe brinjal

**Method:**
1. Rinse the brinjal thoroughly. Remove the ends.
2. Cut the eggplant in half lengthwise.
3. Place the diced pieces in the water-filled bowl.
4. In a saute pan or skillet, heat the oil.
5. Toss in the mustard seeds.
6. Roast for 20 seconds with the urad dal and asafetida.
7. In the same pan, insert the brinjal pieces.
8. Heat the stove to a low heat setting and cover the pan with water.
9. Mix in the salt and onions thoroughly.
10. Shut the cover and continue cooking.

11. Every 2-3 minutes, give it a swirl.
12. Mix in the red chili powder thoroughly.
13. Stir fry for 3-4 minutes more. Turn off the stove.

## 1.16 Indian-Spiced Pickled Vegetables

**Cooking Time:** 30 minutes
**Serving Size:** 4
**Ingredients:**
- ½ cup distilled white vinegar
- 3 tablespoons brown sugar
- 1/3 cup vegetable oil
- 5 dried hot red chili
- ½ seedless cucumber
- ½ teaspoon cumin seeds
- ½ teaspoon fennel seeds
- 1 teaspoon coriander seeds
- 1 teaspoon ground turmeric
- ½ large head cauliflower
- 3 tablespoons peeled ginger
- 1 tablespoon mustard seeds
- 3 tablespoons garlic
- ½ lb. carrots

**Method:**
1. Preheat the oven to 250°F and place the rack in the center.
2. In a big pot of hot simmering water, cook the cabbage and carrots along.
3. Bake, mixing periodically, cabbage, carrots, and celery in a single layer in a shallow baking tray.
4. In a mixing bowl, pulse cloves and spice with one teaspoon of salts until golden brown, then move to a cup.

5. Heat skillet over medium temperature until a drop of water evaporates in a matter of seconds.
6. Pour the oil down the side of the skillet.
7. Cook, mixing, for ten seconds after adding the chili and spice mixture.
8. Heat, constantly stirring, until the garlic paste turns golden, around 15 seconds.
9. Bring the vegetables, mustard, and brown sugar to a boil.
10. Enable to solidify at room temperature in a small bowl.

## 1.17 Cashew Chickpea Curry

**Cooking Time:** 30 minutes
**Serving Size:** 4
   **Ingredients:**
**For the Spice Mix**
- ½ teaspoon turmeric
- 1 green cardamom pod
- ¼ teaspoon nutmeg
- 1 blade mace
- 1½ teaspoons cumin seeds
- ½ teaspoon peppercorns
- ½ teaspoon cinnamon
- 1 whole star anise
- 2 cloves
- 1½ teaspoons coriander seeds

**For the Curry**
- ¼ cup fresh juice limes
- ½ cup fresh cilantro
- 1 bunch spinach leaves
- Kosher salt
- 3 tablespoons vegetable oil
- 1 can coconut milk
- 2 cans chickpeas
- 1 small onion
- ¼ teaspoon cayenne pepper
- ½ cup cashew nuts
- 1 tablespoon ginger
- 1 small red or green chili
- 4 cloves garlic

**Method:**
1. In a seasoning grinder, mix cumin, cilantro, star anise, garlic, peppercorns, cloves, nutmeg, mace, fenugreek, and cinnamon.
2. In a medium skillet, melt the oil, butter, or peanut oil over moderate flame.
3. Combine the onion, garlic, spice, and chili in a large mixing bowl.
4. Add the cayenne pepper, cashews, and half of the spice mixture to the pan.
5. Cook, stirring continuously until the mixture becomes fragrant.
6. Remove the pan from the heat and add the coconut milk.
7. Blend for around thirty seconds or until smooth.
8. Put the mixture back in the pot.
9. Cook, mixing continuously for ten minutes over low heat with chickpeas, broccoli, and the remaining spice mix.
10. To taste, season with salt and lemon juice.
11. Serve with lime slices and curry powder pilaf in a serving dish, topped with extra coriander.

## 1.18 Stir-Fried Chili Greens

**Cooking Time:** 40 minutes
**Serving Size:** 3
**Ingredients:**
- 100g frozen peas
- ½ lemon, juiced
- 1 tablespoon ginger
- 1 red chili
- 1 green chili
- 450g sliced greens
- 1 teaspoon cumin seeds

- 1 teaspoon mustard seeds
- 1 tablespoon vegetable oil

**Method:**
1. In a resealable roasting pan set over a moderate flame, add the oil.
2. Heat for 1 minute after adding the cumin and mustard seeds, then insert the chili and spice and cook for 30 seconds.
3. Combine the vegetables, peas, three tablespoons of water, and a bit of salt in a large mixing bowl.
4. Cook for five minutes with the lid on. To eat, sprinkle with lemon juice.

# Chapter 2: Vegetarian Wok Japanese Recipes

## 2.1 Yasai Itame

**Cooking Time:** 15 minutes
**Serving Size:** 4
   **Ingredients:**
- 1 tablespoon neutral oil
- 3.5 oz. bean sprouts
- 1 clove garlic
- 1 knob ginger
- 6.5 oz. pork
- ¼ cabbage
- ½ carrot
- ¼ onion
- 10 snow peas

**For Pork Marinade**
- 1 teaspoon sake
- 1 teaspoon soy sauce

**For Seasonings**
- Freshly ground black pepper
- 2 teaspoon sesame oil
- 1 teaspoon soy sauce
- ½ teaspoon kosher salt
- 1 teaspoon oyster sauce

**Method:**
1. Slice the vegetables into tiny chunks and sauté them in a shallow saucepan with one teaspoon sesame oil and one teaspoon sake.
2. Start by removing the strings from the green beans and thinly slice the red pepper.
3. Add the ginger and garlic once the wok is warmed.

4. When the meat is fragrant, insert it and prepare until it's around 80% cooked.
5. Stir in the onion and cook until it is almost tender. After that, add the carrots.
6. Combine the broccoli and snow peas in a large mixing bowl.
7. Then throw in the bean sprouts one more period.
8. Combine the oyster sauce and sesame oil in a bowl.
9. Add Salt, fresh roasted black pepper, and two teaspoons of sesame oil to taste.

## 2.2 Japanese Stir-Fried Noodles with Veggies

**Cooking Time:** 30 minutes
**Serving Size:** 3
**Ingredients:**
- 2 teaspoon soy sauce
- 2 teaspoon sugar
- 4 teaspoon oyster sauce
- 4 teaspoon ketchup
- ½ onion
- 1 carrot
- 4-6 tablespoon yakisoba sauce
- 4 tablespoon Worcestershire sauce
- 3 shiitake mushrooms
- Freshly ground black pepper
- 3 servings of yakisoba noodles
- 2 green onions
- ¾ lb. sliced pork belly
- 2 tablespoon neutral-flavored oil
- 4 cabbage leaves

**Method:**
1. Gather all of the necessary ingredients.
2. To make the Yakisoba paste, whisk together all of the components.

3. Break the onion into slices, the carrot into diced pieces, and the shiitake mushrooms into chunks.
4. Heat the oil in a pan or skillet over moderate flame.
5. Cook the vegetables until it is wilted in the center.
6. Cook for 1-2 minutes after adding the onion and carrots.
7. Cook till the cabbage is almost soft.
8. Heat for 1 minute after adding the spring onions and butternut squash.
9. Season with smoked paprika, fresh roasted.
10. Add the Yakisoba Sauce and change the quantity depending on the rest of the ingredients. Serve right away.

## 2.3 Lightly Fried Japanese Vegetables

**Cooking Time:** 50 minutes
**Serving Size:** 4
**Ingredients:**
- Sea salt
- Toasted sesame seeds
- 2 teaspoons mirin
- Sesame oil
- ¼ white cabbage
- 1 tablespoon rice wine vinegar
- 1 tablespoon tamari
- 2 carrots
- 1 small red bell pepper
- 1 small white onion
- 4 spring onions
- 1 zucchini

**Method:**
1. Over medium temperature, heat a big skillet.
2. Add the soy sauce and the veggies once the soy sauce has reached a Smokey flavor.

3. Mix the rice sherry vinegar, tamari, and mirin in a small mixing bowl.
4. To add moisture to the veggies, spray the combination over them when stir-frying.
5. Heat for two minutes, testing to see if the veggies are still crisp.
6. Dress with sea salt if desired, then arrange on serving trays with toasted pine nuts on top.

## 2.4 Vegan Stir-Fried Udon Noodles

**Cooking Time:** 15 minutes
**Serving Size:** 4
**Ingredients:**
- ¼ cup water
- 10.6 ounces Udon noodles
- 1 teaspoon ground ginger
- 4 tablespoon tamari
- 1 tablespoon olive oil
- 1 cup green pepper
- 1 cup carrot
- 1 cup red pepper
- 1 cup onion

**Method:**
1. In a skillet, heat the oil, add vegetables, fresh ginger, 2 tablespoons soya sauce or sesame oil, and liquid.
2. Cook for five minutes on high heat or until the vegetables are cooked.
3. Cook Udon pasta as directed on the box.
4. Two tablespoons of veggie broth or soy sauce, plus the pasta.
5. Cook for another two minutes, stirring occasionally.

## 2.5 Vegetable Yakisoba

**Cooking Time:** 40 minutes
**Serving Size:** 10

### Ingredients:
- 16 oz. yakisoba noodles
- 3 tablespoon oil
- ¼ small cabbage
- 1 large onion
- ½ lb. broccoli
- 2 large carrots
- 1 large sweet bell pepper

### Yakisoba Sauce
- 2 tablespoon ketchup
- 4 tablespoon Worcestershire sauce
- 2 tablespoon soy sauce
- 2 tablespoon oyster sauce
- 2 tablespoon sugar

**Method:**
1. Mix all yakisoba liquid ingredients in a large bowl and set aside.
2. Heat a small amount of oil in a skillet over high heat.
3. Return all of the veggies to the same pan. Separate the noodles as directed on the box. Toss in the noodles in the skillet.
4. Toss all together after pouring the sauce over the components.
5. Reduce the heat to medium-low and cook for five minutes.
6. Take it off the heat and enjoy it!

## 2.6 Hibachi Vegetables

**Cooking Time:** 20 minutes
**Serving Size:** 4
  **Ingredients:**
- ½ teaspoon sesame seeds
- Salt and pepper to taste
- 1 tablespoon soy sauce
- 2 tablespoons teriyaki sauce
- 2 cups broccoli florets
- 8 oz. mushrooms
- 2 tablespoons butter
- 1 zucchini
- 1 cup carrots
- ½ tablespoon garlic
- ½ sweet onion
- 1 tablespoon oil

**Method:**
1. Melt butter in a skillet over medium-high heat, then add the oil and sauté tomatoes and ginger for two minutes, until it's tender.
2. Zucchini, cabbage, lettuce, and mushrooms are all good additions.
3. Dress with salt and pepper to taste after adding the sesame oil and teriyaki sauce.
4. Cook for ten minutes, or until the vegetables are tender.
5. Serve immediately with toasted pine nuts scattered on top.

## 2.7 Wagamama Wok-Fried Greens

**Cooking Time:** 20 minutes
**Serving Size:** 2
  **Ingredients:**
  **For the Sauce**
- 1 tablespoon sesame oil

- Ground black pepper
- 1 teaspoon sugar
- 2 tablespoons soy sauce

**For the Greens**
- 150g tender stem broccoli
- 200g pak choi
- 2 garlic cloves
- 2 tablespoons oil

**Method:**
1. In a small mixing bowl, combine all of the sauce components.
2. In a slow cooker or cooking pan, add the oil.
3. Fry the garlic for about thirty seconds on medium heat until aromatic and golden brown – be careful not to damage it!
4. Combine the broccoli, bok choy, and liquid in a large mixing bowl.
5. Heat, frequently stirring, for around five minutes, or until veggies are cooked to your taste.
6. Taste, and if possible, add more soy sauce.

## 2.8 Vegan Mapo Nasu

**Cooking Time:** 30 minutes
**Serving Size:** 6
**Ingredients:**
- ½ cup slivered scallions
- Cilantro sprigs
- 1 teaspoon Sichuan pepper
- 1 tablespoon corn starch
- 8 ounces shiitake mushrooms
- 2 teaspoons soy sauce
- 1 teaspoon sesame oil
- 2 teaspoons garlic
- 1 tablespoon ginger
- 1 tablespoon black beans
- 1 tablespoon broad bean paste

- 2 cups water
- 3 tablespoons vegetable oil
- 3 small red peppers
- Salt
- 15-ounce soft tofu

**Method:**
1. Mushroom stems should be removed.
2. Simmer the stems in 2 cups water for fifteen minutes to make a light mushrooms soup.
3. Tofu should be sliced into 1-inch pieces.
4. In a pan or a large skillet, heat the oil over medium-high heat.
5. Heat, occasionally stirring, until the red peppers, bean sprouts, and bean paste are spicy, around 1 minute.
6. Stir in the ginger and garlic, and add the mushroom, sesame oil, soy sauce, and Sichuan pepper.
7. Toss in the tofu cubes with care.
8. Sprinkle in the cornstarch combination, stirring the pan gently to mix it.
9. Add green onion and coriander sprigs to finish.

## 2.9 15 Minute Spicy Udon Stir Fry

**Cooking Time:** 15 minutes
**Serving Size:** 2

**Ingredients:**
**Stir Fry**
- 3 cups baby spinach
- 14 oz. soft udon noodles
- 1 medium carrot
- 1 cup green onion
- ½ medium onion
- 1 tablespoon vegetable oil

**Sauce**
- 2 cloves garlic

- 1 teaspoon sesame oil
- 2 tablespoon brown sugar
- 1 tablespoon fresh ginger
- ¼ cup soy sauce
- 2 teaspoon rice wine vinegar
- 2 teaspoon Sambal Oelek

**For Garnish**
- Additional green onion
- ¼ cup parsley
- Sesame seeds

**Method:**
1. Put down your veggies after they've been prepared.
2. In a shallow saucepan, combine all of the ingredients to make the sauce.
3. Heat the oil in a large skillet pot or broiler over medium-high heat until it is hot.
4. Cook, occasionally stirring, for about a minute after adding the carrots.
5. Cook, regularly mixing, until vegetables are soft and carrots are ready.
6. Cook for thirty seconds or so, stirring occasionally.
7. Cook, tossing, for thirty seconds or so after adding the soaked noodles to the wok.
8. Reheat for another thirty seconds, constantly stirring to ensure that everything is well combined.
9. Switch the stir fry to a cup or plate and sprinkle sesame seeds on top.

## 2.10 Stir-Fried Tofu with Vegetables

**Cooking Time:** 50 minutes
**Serving Size:** 4
   **Ingredients:**
   **For Tofu**

- ½ teaspoon black pepper
- 2 tablespoon cornstarch
- 1 tablespoon soy sauce
- 1 tablespoon sesame oil
- 1 block extra-firm tofu

**For Stir Fry**
- 1 red bell pepper
- 2 green onions
- 2 small carrots
- 1 small head of broccoli
- 3 tablespoon olive oil
- 1 tablespoon ginger
- 8 oz. string beans
- 3 cloves garlic
- Kosher salt

**For Sauce**
- 2 tablespoon brown sugar
- 2 teaspoon cornstarch
- 2 teaspoon sesame oil
- ¼ cup water
- 2 tablespoon soy sauce

**Method:**
1. Tofu should be simmered for two minutes in a small saucepan of lightly salted water.
2. Toss tofu in a mixing saucepan with sesame oil, soy sauce, and chili flakes after cutting it into bite-size bits.
3. Add the oil to a large frying pan. Allow tofu to bake.
4. Take from pan and season with salt and pepper before setting aside.
5. Cook until the residual oil is hot, then add the ginger and garlic and fry until aromatic.
6. String bean, broccoli, lettuce, bell pepper, and fresh basil should all be added at this stage. Salt and pepper to taste.

7. Combine soy sauce, soy sauce, water, coconut milk, and cornflour in a small cup.
8. Return the tofu to the skillet and insert the sauce combination.
9. Mix and cook for 2 minutes, or until slightly boiled.

## 2.11 Japanese Mushroom Stir-Fry

**Cooking Time:** 10 minutes
**Serving Size:** 2
  **Ingredients:**
- 2 tablespoon fermented soybeans
- 8 shiitake mushrooms
- 1 small eggplant
- 1 clove garlic
- 2 tablespoon vegetable oil
- 1 x 2cm piece of ginger

**Sauce**
- 1 tablespoon mirin
- 1 tablespoon miso paste
- 1 tablespoon soy sauce
- ½ teaspoon sesame oil
- 2 teaspoon sugar

**Method:**
1. Whisk together all of the sauce components.
2. In a warm skillet, add oil and the garlic and ginger, and fry until translucent.
3. Toss the veggies in the skillet with the oil.
4. Toss in the sliced eggplant and mushrooms for two minutes, just until the eggplant softens.
5. Toss in the liquid, bring to the boil, and toss once more.
6. Turn off the heat after adding the soybeans and tossing them through.
7. Serve hot with beans.

## 2.12 Veggie Stir-Fry Soba Noodle

**Cooking Time:** 15 minutes
**Serving Size:** 1
   **Ingredients:**
- 1 tablespoon Sriracha sauce
- 1 tablespoon creamy nut butter
- 1 large egg
- 1 tablespoon coconut amino
- ¼ cup bell pepper
- ¼ cup broccoli florets
- ½ teaspoon ground ginger
- ¼ cup onion
- ½ tablespoon sesame oil
- ½ teaspoon garlic
- 2 ounces soba noodles

**Method:**
1. Take a medium pot half-filled with water on the stove.
2. Use the soba pasta in the broth.
3. In a medium saucepan, heat the soy sauce over medium-high heat.
4. Combine the ginger, onions, red pepper, garlic, and vegetables in a large mixing bowl.
5. Wrap the pan and bake, stirring periodically, for approximately 3 minutes, or until melted.
6. Strain the soba pasta and toss them in the pan with the veggies.
7. Push all to the sides, cut yolk and white with a fork until scrambled, and then fold into the veggies and pasta.
8. Add in the Sriracha, coconut protein, and almond butter until thoroughly mixed. Heat the pan before serving.

## 2.13 Speedy Japanese Miso Stir Fry & Sticky Rice

**Cooking Time:** 20 minutes
**Serving Size:** 2
   **Ingredients:**
- 90g pack bok choy
- 6 spring onions
- 1 tablespoon sunflower oil
- 250g broccoli
- 1 tablespoon sesame seed
- 1 teaspoon sesame oil
- 140g sushi rice
- 1 tablespoon caster sugar

   **For the Sauce**
- 2 teaspoon ginger
- 1 red chili
- 1 tablespoon rice wine vinegar
- 1 tablespoon soft brown sugar
- 1 tablespoon mirin
- 2 tablespoon brown miso paste

**Method:**
1. Combine all of the sauce components in a mixing bowl with 1 tablespoon water.
2. With the icing salt and sugar, bring a big pot of water to a boil.
3. Cook for fifteen minutes after adding the rice.
4. Cap and keep warm by sprinkling the sesame seeds and sesame oil on top.
5. In a skillet, heat the essential oils until very warm, then mix in the lettuce and stir-fry for three minutes, or until nearly tender, inserting splatters of water to produce steam as required.

6. Cook for another 1-2 minutes after adding the bok choy and spring vegetables, then whisk in the sauce.
7. Divide the rice between two bowls, top with the stir-fry, and serve right away.

## 2.14 Japanese Shrimp & Eggplant Fried Rice

**Cooking Time:** 35 minutes
**Serving Size:** 4
   **Ingredients:**
- 2 cups brown rice
- ¼ cup ponzu sauce
- 2 cups eggplant
- 1 cup shelled edamame
- 2 teaspoons garlic
- 1 pound raw shrimp
- 3 scallions
- 2 teaspoons ginger
- 2 large eggs
- 1 teaspoon peanut oil

**Method:**
1. In a big flat-bottomed wok, warm 1 teaspoon oil.
2. Heat without mixing the eggs.
3. 1 tablespoon oil, green onions, garlic, and cloves in a skillet; cook, swirling, once scallions are soft.
4. Cook for two minutes, stirring constantly.
5. Cook the eggplant and edamame together.
6. Fill a big plate halfway with the contents of the skillet.
7. In the same wok, add the rest one tablespoon oil; add the rice and swirl until it is sweet.
8. Transfer the seafood, vegetables, and shells to the skillet, along with the ponzu sauce, and stir properly.

## 2.15 Vegan Ramen

**Cooking Time:** 20 minutes
**Serving Size:** 3
   **Ingredients:**

- ½ a red pepper
- ½ a zucchini
- 2 carrots
- ½ head of broccoli
- 2 cloves of garlic
- 2 green onions
- 2 tablespoon flavored oil
- 1 tablespoon ginger
- 2 packages of ramen noodles

**For the Stir Fry Sauce**
- 1 tablespoon sriracha
- 1 ½ teaspoons cornstarch
- 3 tablespoons soy sauce
- 1 ½ tablespoons molasses
- 2 tablespoons vegetable stock

**Method:**
1. For the pasta, bring a pot of water to a boil.
2. In the meantime, chop all of your vegetables and mix the stir fry sauce ingredients.
3. Insert the noodles once the water has reached a boil.
4. In a wok or wide pan, add the oil over moderate flame.
5. Combine the ginger, cloves, and the white and light green portions of the spring onions in a mixing bowl.
6. Fry for 10-15 seconds, moving continuously.
7. Combine the broccoli and vegetables in a large mixing bowl.
8. Stir fry until the vegetables start to soften.
9. Continue to stir fry the bell pepper and zucchini.
10. Pour the sauce over the pasta in the bowl.
11. Serve with the green tips of the spring onions.

## 2.16 Vegetable Lo Mein

**Cooking Time:** 25 minutes
**Serving Size:** 4
### Ingredients:
- ½ cup snow peas
- 3 cups baby spinach
- 1 red bell pepper
- 1 carrot
- 8 ounces egg noodles
- 2 cloves garlic
- 2 cups cremini mushrooms
- 1 tablespoon olive oil

### For the Sauce
- ½ teaspoon ground ginger
- ½ teaspoon Sriracha
- 2 teaspoons sugar
- 1 teaspoon sesame oil
- 2 tablespoons soy sauce

**Method:**
1. Set down a bowl full containing sesame oil, sugar, soy sauce, spice, and Sriracha.
2. Heat pasta as per package directions in a large pot of water; rinse well.
3. In a medium saucepan or skillet, heat the olive oil over medium heat.
4. Garlic, onions, red pepper, and carrot are added to the pan.
5. Mix in the green beans and spinach for around 2-3 minutes, or until the kale has ripened.
6. Toss in the egg noodles with the soy sauce combination and toss gently to blend.
7. Serve right away.

## 2.17 Szechuan Eggplant

**Cooking Time:** 45 minutes
**Serving Size:** 4
**Ingredients:**
- 2 teaspoons ginger
- 10 dried red chilies
- 4 tablespoons peanut oil
- 4 cloves garlic
- 2 teaspoons salt
- 2 tablespoons cornstarch
- 1½ lbs. Japanese Eggplant

**Szechuan Sauce**
- 3 tablespoons sugar
- ½ teaspoon five-spice
- 1 tablespoon rice vinegar
- 1 tablespoon cooking wine
- 1 teaspoon Szechuan peppercorns
- 1 tablespoon garlic chili paste
- 1 tablespoon sesame oil
- ¼ cup soy sauce

**Method:**
1. Cut the eggplant into ½ inch slices.
2. Place in a large mixing bowl with two teaspoons salts and fill with water.
3. Meanwhile, finely cut the ginger and garlic.
4. In a dry pan, toast the Szechuan peppers.
5. In a small cup, whisk together these and the leftover marinade.
6. Combine the eggplant and corn starch in a mixing bowl.
7. In an extra-large pan, heat 1 to 2 teaspoons oil over moderate flame.
8. Half of the eggplant should be spread out.
9. Add one tablespoon of further oil to the skillet and cook the ginger and garlic for two minutes over low heat, stirring constantly.

10. Serve in a casserole plate with shallots on top.

# Chapter 3: Vegetarian Wok Chinese Recipes

## 3.1 Saucy Vegetable Stir Fry

**Cooking Time:** 15 minutes
**Serving Size:** 4
  **Ingredients:**
- 1 cup mushrooms
- 1 capsicum
- 1 carrot
- 3 medium bok choy
- 1 tablespoon vegetable oil
- 1 tablespoon ginger
- ½ onion
- 2 garlic cloves

**Sauce**
- Dash of white pepper
- ¾ cup water
- 1 tablespoon Chinese cooking wine
- ½ teaspoon sesame oil
- 1½ tablespoon soy sauce
- 2 teaspoon Oyster Sauce
- 1 tablespoon cornflour

**Method:**
1. In a mixing bowl, whisk together the cornflour and soy sauce till the cornflour is dissolved completely, then add the remaining sauce components.
2. In a skillet or a large heavy-bottomed skillet, heat the oil over medium temperature.
3. Stir in the ginger and garlic for ten seconds.
4. Stir in the onion for thirty seconds.
5. Stir in the carrots, bell pepper, and bok choy stems for two minutes.

6. Mix in the mushrooms for two or three minutes, or until the veggies are almost finished.
7. Toss in the Sauce for two minutes, or until it thickens and becomes shiny.
8. Remove the pan from the heat and serve over rice.

## 3.2 Vegetable Stir-Fry Noodles

**Cooking Time:** 10 minutes
**Serving Size:** 2
**Ingredients:**
- 2 tablespoon soy sauce
- 1 teaspoon white wine vinegar
- 2 spring onions
- 85g beansprout
- 150g pack egg noodle
- 1 yellow pepper
- 100g mange tout
- 1 tablespoon vegetable oil
- 2 garlic cloves
- 1 large carrot
- 2.5cm ginger

**Method:**
1. Cook the noodles as directed on the package.
2. In a griddle or large deep fryer, add the oil, whisk the onion, ginger, cabbage, peppers, mange tout, sweet snap, or green beans for 2-3 minutes over medium temperature.
3. Drain the pasta thoroughly, then stir-fry for two minutes with the vegetables and beansprouts, if using.
4. Combine the sesame oil and mustard in a bowl and stir into the dish.
5. Serve immediately after dividing between plates.

## 3.3 Ginger Veggie Stir Fry

**Cooking Time:** 40 minutes
**Serving Size:** 6
  **Ingredients:**
- ¼ cup onion
- ½ tablespoon salt
- 2 tablespoons soy sauce
- 2 ½ tablespoons water
- ¾ cup carrots
- ½ cup green beans
- 1 tablespoon cornstarch
- 1 small head of broccoli
- ½ cup snow peas
- 1 ½ cloves garlic
- ¼ cup vegetable oil
- 2 teaspoons ginger root

**Method:**
1. Mix cornflour, cloves, one teaspoon ginger, and two tablespoons of veggie butter in a pan mixing bowl until cornstarch is absorbed.
2. Toss in the tomatoes, snow peas, vegetables, and sweet potatoes, lightly coating them.
3. In a medium saucepan or Dutch oven, heat the remaining two tablespoons of oil over medium-high heat.
4. Cook for an additional minute in oil with the vegetables.
5. Combine the soy sauce and liquid in a mixing bowl.
6. Combine the onion, salt, and the leftover one teaspoon ginger in a mixing bowl.
7. Cook until the veggies are soft but still crispy, about 10 minutes.

## 3.4 Stir-Fried Lettuce with Garlic Chiles

**Cooking Time:** 15 minutes
**Serving Size:** 3
   **Ingredients:**
- 2 teaspoons oyster sauce
- 1 teaspoon salt
- 4 cloves garlic
- 1 head romaine lettuce
- 2 spring onions
- 1 ½ tablespoon vegetable oil

**Method:**
1. In a slow cooker or big skillet, add the oil over medium heat and add the spring onions and half of the seasoning.
2. Continue cooking for 1 minute, or until moist.
3. Continue cooking in the romaine lettuce and miso paste until the basil turns greenish.
4. Reduce the heat to moderate.
5. Stir in the leftover garlic and salt to the lettuce combination.

## 3.5 Wok Black Bean Glaze and Tossed Veggies in Honey Recipe

**Cooking Time:** 25 minutes
**Serving Size:** 4
   **Ingredients:**
- 1 tablespoon honey
- 1 teaspoon black pepper
- 1 ½ teaspoon bean and garlic paste
- ½ lime
- 4-5 sweet gourds
- 4-5 water chestnuts
- 1 teaspoon soya sauce
- 1 medium Chinese cabbage

- To taste salt
- 4-5 shitake mushrooms
- 1 teaspoon ginger
- 1 bok choy

**Method:**
1. In a skillet, put a tablespoon of oil, transfer all the diced vegetables to it.
2. Season with salt and pepper.
3. Water cucumbers and shitake mushrooms should be added at this stage.
4. Vegetable oil, sweet potato and garlic paste, ½ lime juice, sugar, and crushed black pepper are added.
5. In a skillet, mix thoroughly for around 4-5 minutes. Serve immediately.

## 3.6 Shrimp and Chinese Vegetable Stir-Fry

**Cooking Time:** 10 minutes
**Serving Size:** 3

**Ingredients:**
- 3 button mushrooms
- 6 snow peas
- ¼ yellow bell pepper
- 4 asparagus
- 20 shrimp
- A small pinch of salt
- ½ tablespoon sesame oil
- Three tablespoons vegetable cooking oil
- 1 tablespoon fish sauce
- 2 cloves garlic

**Marinating**
- ¼ teaspoon sugar
- ¼ teaspoon ground white pepper
- ¼ teaspoon salt

**Method:**
1. Devein the shrimp and season with salt, sea salt, and sugar before marinating.
2. In a slow cooker, heat about two tablespoons of sunflower oil and cook the seafood until they turn color.
3. In the remaining one tablespoon of sunflower oil, cook the garlic until fragrant.
4. Place the mushroom and red pepper in the oven for about a half-minute or until soft and mildly seared.
5. Asparagus and winter bean pieces should be added at this stage.
6. Add a pinch of salt to taste.
7. Return the seafood to the pan with the curry powder and sesame oil drizzled on top.
8. Fry quickly and remove from the pan as soon as possible.

## 3.7 Black Bean Sauce with Stir Fry Veggies

**Cooking Time:** 30 minutes
**Serving Size:** 4
   **Ingredients:**
**Black Bean Sauce**
- 1 tablespoon brown sugar
- 1 teaspoon chili garlic sauce
- 1 tablespoon rice cooking wine
- 1 tablespoon water
- 2 tablespoon garlic sauce

**Vegetables**
- 2 small zucchini
- 2 bulbs bok choy
- 2 cloves garlic
- ½ large red bell pepper
- 3 tablespoon avocado oil
- 1 large carrot

- 1 teaspoon fresh ginger
- 3 green onions
- 1 large Chinese eggplant

**Method:**
1. Combine packaged sweet chili sauce, rice cooking liquor, water, coconut milk, and chili garlic sauce in a small cup.
2. Preheat the oven to 350°F and a large pan to a moderate flame.
3. In a flour mixture, combine the eggplant and one tablespoon of oil.
4. In a hot oven skillet, add the eggplant. Sauté until the vegetables are soft and golden brown.
5. Heat the remaining oil in the same pan.
6. Green onion, broccoli, pepper, and garlic are all good additions.
7. Sauté the bell pepper, zucchini, and scallions until soft, stirring occasionally.
8. Return the eggplant to the veggies, stir in the black bean sauce, reduce the heat to low, and continue to cook for a few minutes.
9. Serve over potatoes, Asian noodles, or zoodles while still warm.

## 3.8 Spring Veggie Stir-Fry

**Cooking Time:** 20 minutes
**Serving Size:** 4
**Ingredients:**
- Pinch of salt
- ½ bunch thin asparagus
- 1 small red onion
- 3 medium carrots
- ¼ cup soy sauce
- ½ teaspoon red pepper
- 1 tablespoon coconut oil
- 2 tablespoons honey

- 1 tablespoon ginger
- 1 large clove garlic
- 2 teaspoons arrowroot starch

**Method:**
1. Mix the sesame oil, sugar, cornflour, spice, garlic, and bell pepper flakes in a fluid measuring cup.
2. Preheat oil in a medium saucepan until it shimmers.
3. With a sprinkle of flour, toss in the onion and carrots.
4. Heat, mixing every 30 seconds, till the carrots begin to caramelize, then add the asparagus.
5. Pour in the ready sauce and cook for 30 to 60 seconds, stirring frequently.
6. Remove from the heat and season with salt, fried eggs, or tofu.

## 3.9 Chinese Cabbage Stir-Fry

**Cooking Time:** 15 minutes
**Serving Size:** 4

**Ingredients:**
- 1 tablespoon soy sauce
- 1 tablespoon Chinese cooking wine
- 2 cloves garlic
- 1 pound cabbage
- 1 tablespoon vegetable oil

**Method:**
1. In a slow cooker or large pan, heat the peanut oil over medium-high heat.
2. Cook for a few minutes, constantly stirring, before the garlic starts to brown.
3. Close the skillet and continue cooking after stirring in the broccoli until it is fully coated in oil.
4. Continue cooking for the next minute after adding the soy sauce.
5. Mix in the Chinese cooking wine and raise the heat to be heavy.

6. Cook and stir for another two minutes, or until the cabbage is soft.

## 3.10 Veggie and Tofu Stir-Fry

**Cooking Time:** 50 minutes
**Serving Size:** 4
  **Ingredients:**
  **For Tofu**
- ½ teaspoon black pepper
- 2 tablespoon cornstarch
- 1 tablespoon soy sauce
- 1 tablespoon sesame oil
- 1 (14-oz.) block tofu

**For Stir Fry**
- 1 red bell pepper
- 2 green onions
- 2 small carrots
- 1 small head of broccoli
- 1 tablespoon ginger
- 8 oz. string beans
- Kosher salt
- 3 cloves garlic
- 3 tablespoon olive oil

**For Sauce**
- 2 tablespoon packed brown sugar
- 2 teaspoon cornstarch
- 2 teaspoon sesame oil
- ¼ cup water
- 2 tablespoon l soy sauce

**Method:**
1. Tofu should be simmered for two minutes in a small saucepan of salted boiling water.
2. Slice tofu into bite-size bits and combine in a mixing saucepan with sesame oil, soy sauce, and garlic powder.
3. In a large frying pan, heat two tablespoons of oil.
4. Allow tofu to fry. Salt and pepper to taste.

5. Cook the ginger and garlic in the leftover one tablespoon oil until aromatic.
6. String beans, broccoli, kale, bell pepper, and fresh basil should all be added at this stage.
7. Heat for 10 minutes, or until the vegetables are tender. Salt and pepper to taste.
8. Combine sesame oil, soy sauce, water, coconut milk, and cornflour in a small cup.
9. Stir and continue cooking, or until moderately thickened.

## 3.11 Seitan Stir-Fry and Vegan Chinese Vegetable Recipe

**Cooking Time:** 25 minutes
**Serving Size:** 4
   **Ingredients:**
   **For the Stir-Fry Sauce**
   - 2 teaspoons corn starch
   - ½ tablespoon dark soy sauce
   - 2 teaspoons sesame oil
   - 2 teaspoons maple syrup
   - 1 tablespoon Shaoxing wine
   - 2 tablespoons soy sauce
   
   **For the Stir-Fry**
   - 1 medium red pepper
   - 1 medium carrot
   - 4 cloves garlic
   - 1 head broccoli
   - 1 medium red onion
   - 1 portion seitan

**Method:**
1. To make the sauce, combine all of the ingredients.
2. Preheat a large nonstick skillet. One tablespoon balanced oil of choice.
3. Fry until the seitan is neatly caramelized and crispy around the edges.

4. In the same pan, heat another 12 tablespoons of oil and add the onion, sautéing for 3-4 minutes.
5. Heat for another two minutes after adding the garlic.
6. Combine the lettuce, cabbage, and red pepper in a large mixing bowl.
7. Cook for five minutes, or until the vegetables are tender.
8. Finally, return the seitan to the pot with the stir-fry liquid.
9. Toss until all of the sauce has been dispersed equally.

## 3.12 Tofu Stir-Fry with Garlic Sauce

**Cooking Time:** 30 minutes
**Serving Size:** 4
  **Ingredients:**
  **For the Sauce**
- 1 teaspoon sesame oil
- 1 tablespoon cornstarch
- 1 teaspoon ginger
- 2 teaspoons sriracha sauce
- 2 tablespoons water
- 4 garlic cloves
- 2 tablespoons rice vinegar
- 2 tablespoons maple syrup
- ¼ cup soy sauce

  **For the Tofu Stir-Fry**
- 1 medium broccoli crown
- 4 ounces shiitake mushroom
- 3 scallions
- 1 medium carrot
- 1 (14 ounces) package tofu
- 1 tablespoon canola oil

**Method:**
1. In a small mixing bowl, combine the sauce ingredients.
2. In a skillet, add the tofu squares.
3. Tofu should be cooked for about ten minutes.
4. Move the tofu to a tray after removing it from the pan.
5. Increase the temperature to high.
6. In a skillet, combine the white pieces of the shallots and the carrots.
7. 1 minute of stir-frying.
8. In the same skillet, add the kale and mushrooms. Stir-fry for another two or three minutes.
9. Apply the sauces to the tofu and return it to the pan.
10. Take the pan from the pan and add the scallions' green bits.
11. Serve on plates with sesame oil on top. Serve with a side of rice.

## 3.13 Chinese Broccoli with Oyster Sauce

**Cooking Time:** 8 minutes
**Serving Size:** 2
  **Ingredients:**
- 1 bunch Chinese broccoli

**Oyster Sauce**
- 1 clove garlic
- 1 teaspoon ginger
- ½ tablespoon vegetable oil
- ½ teaspoon sugar
- 1 tablespoon Chinese cooking wine
- ½ teaspoon sesame oil
- ¾ teaspoon cornflour
- 2 tablespoon oyster sauce
- 2 teaspoon soy sauce
- 3 tablespoon water

**Method:**
1. Remove the ends of the Chinese Broccoli.
2. Combine liquid and corn starch in a medium bowl, mix to absorb.
3. Then add the rest and bring to the boil on medium heat.
4. Remove from heat after 30 seconds to allow the sauce to stiffen.
5. Serve with a drizzle of sesame oil over Chinese broccoli.
6. It is best served hot.

## 3.14 Ramen Stir Fry

**Cooking Time:** 30 minutes
**Serving Size:** 4
**Ingredients:**
- 2 green onions
- ½ teaspoon sesame seeds
- 3 cloves garlic
- 1 tablespoon ginger
- 2 (3.5-ounce) ramen noodles
- 1 pound lean beef
- 1 cup diced sweet onion
- 1 teaspoon Sriracha
- 1 tablespoon sesame oil
- ¼ cup oyster sauce
- 1 tablespoon rice wine vinegar
- 1/3 cup beef stock

**Method:**
1. Stir fry ramen pasta until soft in a big pot of water.
2. Mix vegetable stock, oyster sauce, rice vinegar, and Sriracha in a medium mixing bowl.
3. In a medium saucepan, heat soy sauce over medium-high heat.

4. Cook, occasionally stirring, until the ground beef has golden brown, about 3-5 minutes.
5. One minute after adding the garlic and ginger, mix until aromatic.
6. Scrape any browned bits from the lower part of the skillet before adding the beef stock blend.
7. About 1-2 minutes after adding the ramen noodles, stir until they are heated through it and equitably coated in sauce.
8. Mix thoroughly with spring onions and sesame seeds as a garnish.

## 3.15 Chinese Fried Rice

**Cooking Time:** 30 minutes
**Serving Size:** 4
  **Ingredients:**
- 3 large eggs
- Thinly sliced green onions
- 2 cloves garlic
- 2 tablespoon soy sauce
- 1 cup rice
- 1 large carrot
- 1 ½ cup frozen peas
- 1 tablespoon. sesame oil
- 1 large onion
- Kosher salt

**Method:**
1. Take 2 cups of water and brown rice to a boil in a small saucepan.
2. Cover and simmer for 20 minutes, or until all of the water has been absorbed.
3. Fluff with a fork after seasoning with salt.
4. Add the oil to a large frying pan.
5. Cook, occasionally stirring, until the onion, carrot, and peas are tender around 10 to 15 minutes.
6. Cook for another minute until the garlic and soy sauces are fragrant.
7. Scramble the eggs for 1 to 2 minutes.
8. Three minutes after adding the cooked rice, heat thoroughly.
9. Cover with spring onions and rain of sesame oil.

## 3.16 Cashew Stir Fry Kale Mushroom

**Cooking Time:** 10 minutes
**Serving Size:** 2
  **Ingredients:**
- 1 teaspoon Chinese five-spice
- 1 tablespoon soy sauce
- 1 cup peas
- ¼ cup raw cashew nuts
- 2-3 teaspoons groundnut oil
- 170g mushrooms
- 225g kale
- 1 red chili
- 1 small piece of ginger

**Method:**
1. In a large nonstick skillet, heat the oil.
2. Combine the ginger, chili, and mushrooms in a bowl.
3. Fry for a total of two minutes.
4. Toss in the kale and lentils. Cook for a total of two minutes.
5. Heat for two minutes after adding the cashews.
6. Toss in the five-spice powder and soy sauce in the pan.
7. Toss with the remaining ingredients, heat through, and serve.

## 3.17 Vegetables in Hot Garlic Sauce

**Cooking Time:** 20 minutes
**Serving Size:** 4
  **Ingredients:**
  **Hot Garlic Sauce**
- 1 teaspoon red chili flakes
- ¼ cup red chili sauce
- 1 tablespoon sugar
- 2 tablespoon soy sauce

**Vegetables**
- 1 cup baby corn
- 1 cup zucchini
- 1 cup red bell pepper
- 1 cup mushrooms
- 1 cup green capsicum
- 1 cup yellow bell pepper
- 1 large-size onion, diced

**Other Ingredients**
- 2 tablespoon cornflour
- 4 cup water
- Salt to taste
- ½ teaspoon black pepper
- 4 whole dry red chilies
- 2 tablespoon white vinegar
- 4 tablespoon sesame oil
- 1 tablespoon ginger
- 2 tablespoon celery
- Ten garlic cloves
- 2 tablespoon cooking oil

**Method:**
1. Vegetables should be washed, cleaned, and chopped.
2. ½ cup water to dissolve the cornflour
3. Brown sugar, red chili flakes, sesame oil, and Sriracha sauce should all be combined.
4. In a wok or boil pan, heat the olive oil.
5. Stir-fry all of the veggies, except the onion, for 1 to 2 minutes at medium temperature.
6. In the same skillet, heat soy sauce.
7. Garlic, whole red bell peppers, ginger, and celery, thinly sliced
8. Stir in the diced onion and cook for a few minutes.
9. Pour in the white vinegar and stir well.
10. After that, add the hot garlic seasoning mix that has been prepared.

11. To combine, stir everything together. Salt and black pepper to taste.
12. Add green onions, crushed peanuts, and red chili to the gravy as a garnish.

## 3.18 Stir-Fried Chinese Egg Noodles with Oyster Sauce

**Cooking Time:** 20 minutes
**Serving Size:** 2
　**Ingredients:**
- 2 tablespoon vegetable oil
- To taste black pepper
- 1 teaspoon sesame oil
- 1 teaspoon sesame seeds
- 1 tablespoon soy sauce
- 1 teaspoon fish sauce
- 1 package (12.5 oz.) egg noodles
- 1 large clove garlic
- 2 tablespoon oyster sauce
- 6 Brussels sprouts
- 1/3 cup carrots
- ½ small onion
- ½ cup green beans

**Method:**
1. In a huge nonstick pan or skillet, pour the olive oil and heat it over medium-high heat.
2. After that, combine the Brussels sprouts, parsley, and onion in a mixing bowl.
3. Cook the veggies for 40 seconds on low heat.
4. Green beans and carrots should be added to the pan.
5. Then add the oyster sauce, sesame oil, soy sauce, and fish sauce to the veggies.
6. Cook for the next minute after stirring the vegetables thoroughly.
7. Add the egg noodles to the pot.

8. Remove the stir-fried Chinese rice noodles and veggies from the wok and place them in large bowls.

# Chapter 4: Vegetarian Wok Thai Recipes

## 4.1 Thai Stir-Fried Vegetables with Garlic, Ginger, and Lime

**Cooking Time:** 20 minutes
**Serving Size:** 6
  **Ingredients:**
- Fresh coriander
- Cashew nuts
- Baby corn
- Sesame oil
- Bamboo shoots
- Water chestnuts
- 1 red capsicum
- 3 cups bok choy
- 6 shiitake mushrooms
- 1 small head of broccoli
- ¼ cup shallots
- 1 fresh chili
- 1 carrot, sliced
- 2 thumb size ginger
- 6 cloves garlic

**Stir-Fry Sauce**
- ½ teaspoon dry chili flakes
- 2½ teaspoons brown sugar
- 3½ tablespoons lime juice
- 1½ tablespoons soy sauce
- 2½ tablespoons fish sauce
- 400ml coconut milk

**Method:**
1. In a cup or pan, mix all of the components for the stir fry sauce.
2. To remove the sugar, stir vigorously.

3. In a hot wok, pour in the oil.
4. Combine the shallot, garlic, ginger, and chili in a large mixing bowl.
5. Add the carrots and mushrooms, as well as a quarter of the sauce mixture.
6. ½ of the remaining sauce, tomatoes, bell pepper, and bamboo shoots
7. Insert the bok choy and as well as residual sauce.
8. Wrap up the dish with a generous sprinkling of cashew nuts.

## 4.2 Thai Stir-Fried Mixed Vegetables Recipe

**Cooking Time:** 40 minutes
**Serving Size:** 4
**Ingredients:**
- Thai chilies
- 1 teaspoon sugar
- 5 shiitake mushrooms
- 5 cloves garlic
- 3 stalks Chinese broccoli
- 10 sugar snap peas
- 2 tablespoon oyster sauce
- ¼ head cauliflower
- 3 cups cabbage
- 2 teaspoon soy sauce
- 1 tablespoon water
- ½ cup carrots
- 2 teaspoon golden mountain sauce

**Method:**
1. Combine oyster sauce, sesame oil, golden mountains seasoning, and water in a small cup.
2. Combine the carrot and cabbage in a mixing dish.
3. Later, add the cabbage, snap beans, gai lan roots, and mushroom.
4. Switch the medium heat in a skillet or a big sauté pan, insert a little vegetable oil, onions, bell peppers, and sauté.
5. Toss in the carrots and cauliflower for around two minutes over medium heat.
6. Insert bowl 2 of veggies.
7. Toss until the veggies are almost completed to your taste.
8. Add gai lan leaf, toss just until softened.

# 4.3 Vegetarian Thai Noodles

**Cooking Time:** 15 minutes
**Serving Size:** 4
  **Ingredients:**
  **For the Pad Thai**
- ½ cup peanuts
- ½ cup fresh herbs
- 2 tablespoons oil
- 1 egg, beaten
- 4 ounces brown rice noodles
- Half a yellow onion
- 2 carrots
- 1 red pepper
- 1 zucchini

  **For the Sauce**
- 1 tablespoon soy sauce
- 1 teaspoon chili paste
- 3 tablespoons vegetable broth
- 2 tablespoons white vinegar
- 3 tablespoons brown sugar
- 3 tablespoons fish sauce

**Method:**
1. To soak the undercooked noodles, place them in a bowl of ice water.
2. In a pan, mix the sauce ingredients and shake well.
3. Over medium-high pressure, heat a tablespoon of oil.
4. Stir in the vegetables and cook for a few minutes.
5. Add a further tablespoon of oil to a pan.
6. Add the pasta to the hot pan and stir fry for just a moment, using tweezers to toss.
7. Mix in the liquid for another couple of minutes, just until the sauce begins to thicken and adhere to the noodles.

8. With both the tongs, flip it around. The egg combination will cling to the noodles, causing them to become sticky.
9. Remove from heat after adding the veggies and tossing them together.

## 4.4 Easy Thai Basil Vegetable Stir Fry

**Cooking Time:** 25 minutes
**Serving Size:** 4
  **Ingredients:**
- 3 carrots
- 3 cups Thai basil
- 1 bell pepper
- 2 cups snap peas
- 1 cup uncooked rice
- 2 tablespoon coconut oil
- 1 head broccoli
- 3 large garlic cloves

**For the Sauce**
- ½ teaspoon sesame oil
- 1 tablespoon coconut sugar
- 1 tablespoon fish sauce
- 2 tablespoon rice vinegar
- 2 tablespoon tamari

**Method:**
1. Cook rice according to package directions and set aside.
2. Mix all seasoning ingredients in a small bowl and set aside.
3. Melt the coconut oil in a large saucepan over medium heat.
4. Add garlic and simmer for one moment.
5. It should turn a golden brown color but not burn. Keep a close eye on things.
6. Broccoli, red pepper, peas, and vegetables are all good additions.

7. Enable 3 minutes for the vegetables to steam.
8. Stir in the basil and cook for another 1-2 minutes, or until the basil has wilted.

## 4.5 Spicy Thai Basil Fried Rice

**Cooking Time:** 40 minutes
**Serving Size:** 6
**Ingredients:**
- 1 cucumber
- ½ cup cilantro sprigs
- 1 onion
- 2 cups sweet Thai basil
- 1 red pepper
- 6 large cloves garlic clove
- 2 serrano peppers
- 3 tablespoons oyster sauce
- ½ cup peanut oil
- 4 cups jasmine rice
- 1 teaspoon white sugar
- 2 tablespoons fish sauce

**Method:**
1. In a mixing bowl, combine the oyster sauce, shrimp paste, and sugar.
2. In a skillet, add the oil over a moderate flame until it begins to start smoking.
3. Add the onion and chilies peppers, mixing quickly.
4. Mix in the green pepper, onion, and oyster sauce combination; cook.
5. Boost the heat to maximum and rapidly stir in the cooled rice, blending the sauce into the rice.
6. Remove the pan from the heat and add the spring onions.
7. As needed, garnish with shredded cabbage and coriander.

## 4.6 Thai Vegetable Fried Rice with Cashews

**Cooking Time:** 30 minutes
**Serving Size:** 6
  **Ingredients:**
- ½ lime
- 2 tablespoon Thai basil
- 4 cup broccoli florets
- 1 cup sweet peas frozen
- 1 tablespoon brown sugar
- 4 cup jasmine rice
- 1 cup cashews
- 4 tablespoon tamari divided
- 2 tablespoon liquid amino
- 5 tablespoon sesame oil
- 1 tablespoon fresh ginger
- 2 teaspoon red chili pepper flakes
- 1½ cup yellow onion
- 1 cup red bell pepper
- 1 tablespoon fresh garlic
- 1 cup shiitake

**Method:**
1. Heat the oven to 350F. In a cookie sheet, put the cashews and cook for 12-14 minutes.
2. Warm the sesame oil in a big Dutch oven until it shimmers.
3. Add the mushrooms to the vegetables and stir fry for two minutes.
4. Mix in the bell peppers with the mushrooms and vegetables for another two minutes.
5. On medium-low heat, add the onion, spice, and red pepper flakes to the vegetables' combination and cook for one minute.
6. Transfer the broccoli and green peas to the rice combination.

7. Stir until all of the vegetables are distributed equally.
8. Place the rice in large bowls and top with green onions, sesame seeds, additional herbs, and lime sliders.

## 4.7 Vegetarian Thai Yellow Curry

**Cooking Time:** 30 minutes
**Serving Size:** 4
Ingredients:
Curry
- ¼ cup roasted cashews
- 1 medium lemon
- ¼ cup green peas
- 2 ripe mangos
- 1 ½ tablespoon coconut oil
- 1 teaspoon ground turmeric
- 1 red bell pepper
- 1 medium shallot
- ¼ teaspoon sea salt
- 2-3 teaspoon tamari
- 2 tablespoon fresh ginger
- 2 14-ounce coconut milk
- 3 tablespoon coconut sugar
- 2 cloves minced garlic
- 1 cup chopped red cabbage
- 3 tablespoon red curry paste
- 1 Thai red chili

**Method:**
1. Over medium-high heat, heat a big cast-iron skillet.
2. Add the coconut oil, red onion, carrot, cloves, and peppers once the pan is warmed.
3. Add a pinch of salt and cook, constantly stirring, for three minutes.

4. Stir in the cabbage and red curry spice, and bake for another two minutes.
5. Stir in coconut milk, maple syrup, sea salt, soya sauce, and turmeric.
6. Reduce heat to low and add bell pepper and peas.
7. Heat, stirring periodically, for 5-ten minutes to soften the peppers and peas and incorporate them with curry flavor.
8. After the broth has been well-seasoned and the peppers have lightened, add the mango, cashew nuts, and lime juice and continue to cook for 3-4 minutes.
9. Serve with steamed broccoli and rice or coconut brown rice.

## 4.8 Thai Satay Stir-Fry

**Cooking Time:** 10 minutes
**Serving Size:** 4
**Ingredients:**
- Handful basil leaves
- 25g roasted peanuts
- Thumb-sized root ginger
- 300g pack stir-fry vegetable
- 300g pack noodle
- 1 tablespoon oil
- 3 tablespoon sweet chili sauce
- 2 tablespoon soy sauce
- 3 tablespoon peanut butter

**Method:**
1. To form a delicious satay sauce, combine the peanut butter, chili sauce, water, and sesame oil.
2. Place the pasta in a bowl and cover it with boiling water.
3. To detach, softly stir, then wash completely.
4. In a skillet, heat the oil, then whisk the herb and the tougher vegetables.

5. Stir in the pasta and the remaining vegetables for 1-2 minutes over medium temperature or until the veggies are just fried.
6. Place the vegetables on one side of the pan and the bean paste on the other.
7. Bring the water to a boil. To serve, combine the sauce with the stir-fry, then top with spring onions and peanuts.

## 4.9 Vegetarian Pad See Ew with Tofu and Chinese Eggplant

**Cooking Time:** 30 minutes
**Serving Size:** 4
  **Ingredients:**
- 12 oz. broccoli
- 2 large eggs, beaten
- 2 cloves garlic
- 1 tablespoon water
- 3 tablespoons canola oil
- ⅓ cup shallot
- 2 tablespoons dark soy sauce
- 16 oz. extra firm tofu
- 1 lb. rice noodle
- 1 tablespoon light brown sugar
- 1 teaspoon Thai chili powder
- 3 tablespoons oyster sauce

**Method:**
1. Mix the sesame oil, vegan oyster sauce, coconut milk, and chili powder in a small cup.
2. Drizzle 2 teaspoons of the sauce over the tofu in a medium dish.
3. In a wide nonstick skillet, heat two tablespoons of oil, circling the pot to coat it.
4. In the same pan, add the rest tablespoon of olive oil.

5. Heat until the shallots are soft and golden brown in the pan.
6. Heat for thirty seconds, or until the garlic and water are fragrant.
7. Heat, sometimes tossing, until the Chinese broccoli is tender.
8. Toss in the stored rice noodles, tofu, and sauces until all is well combined.
9. Toss the eggs with the rest of the ingredients to combine them.

## 4.10 Veggie Thai Red Curry

**Cooking Time:** 20 minutes
**Serving Size:** 4
### Ingredients:
- 1 teaspoon brown sugar
- Jasmine rice
- 140g sugar snap pea
- 20g pack basil
- ½ red pepper
- 140g mushrooms
- 200g firm tofu, cubed
- 1 courgette
- 1 small aubergine
- 2 tablespoon vegetable oil
- 400ml can coconut milk
- Juice 3 limes
- 2 red chilies
- 4-5 tablespoon soy sauce

### For the Paste
- 1 teaspoon pepper
- 1 teaspoon ground coriander
- Thumb-size piece ginger
- 2 garlic cloves
- Zest 1 lime
- Stalks coriander

- 3 red chilies
- 3 shallots
- ½ red pepper
- 1 lemongrass

**Method:**
1. In a mixing bowl, combine the paste components.
2. Toss the tofu with two tablespoons of sesame oil, one lemon juice, and chopped chili.
3. In a wide pan, heat half of the oil. Fry 3-4 tablespoons of paste.
4. Cook for ten minutes after adding the cocoa powder, water, aubergine, courgette, and pepper.
5. Drain the tofu, pat it dry, and then fry it until crispy in a shallow saucepan with the cooking liquid.
6. Toss in the onions, sugar snap peas, and the majority of the herbs.
7. Cook until the mushrooms are soft, about three minutes.
8. Serve with rice noodles and garnished with sliced chili and basil.

## 4.11 Easy Vegetable Stir Fry with Creamy Peanut Sauce

**Cooking Time:** 25 minutes
**Serving Size:** 2
**Ingredients:**
**For the Peanut Sauce**
- ¼ cup water
- 1 tablespoon maple syrup
- 2 tablespoon soy sauce
- 2 tablespoon sweet chili sauce
- 2 tablespoon peanut butter

**For the Stir-Fry**
- 3.5 oz. noodles
- 1 handful peanuts

- 1 big handful of snow peas
- 6-8 baby corns
- 1 tablespoon peanut oil
- 1 onion
- 2-3 cups vegetables
- 1 piece ginger
- 1 clove garlic

**Method:**
1. Gather all of the ingredients and place them in one location.
2. Put the peanut butter, sesame oil, sweet chili sauce, liquid, and syrup in a large mixing bowl.
3. Then use a spoon, thoroughly combine the ingredients.
4. Prepare the noodles.
5. Add the oil in a sauté pan or large skillet until it begins to smoke.
6. Combine the garlic, spice, onion, candy snaps, and green beans in a large mixing bowl.
7. After about 40 seconds, add the defrosted vegetables.
8. For around 4-5 minutes, vigorously stir it.
9. Reduce the heat to medium-low and stir in the sauce and pasta.
10. Check to see if everything is smooth and creamy.
11. Allow for another 3-5 minutes of simmering.
12. Before eating, remove the thyme.

## 4.12 Thai Morning Glory Stir Fry

**Cooking Time:** 5 minutes
**Serving Size:** 4
   **Ingredients:**
- ½ tablespoon oyster sauce
- 1 tablespoon vegetable oil
- ½ tablespoon soybean paste
- ½ tablespoon soy sauce
- 4 Thai hot chili
- 3 large cloves of garlic
- 1 bunch water morning glory

**Method:**
1. Put the morning glory in a container and break it into 4 inch long parts.
2. Then weigh the sauce ingredients and add them to the bowl as well.
3. Add the garlic and bell peppers to the edge of the dish, broken up.
4. In a large skillet, add the oil until it is very warm, then insert the container's components all at once.
5. Mix and fry rapidly till the morning glory is softened, having to turn for the lower part.

## 4.13 Thai Combination Fried Rice

**Cooking Time:** 20 minutes
**Serving Size:** 4
   **Ingredients:**
- 2 eggs
- 3 cups cooked jasmine rice
- 5 oz. prawns
- 3 green onion
- 2 large garlic cloves

- ½ onion
- 2 tablespoon vegetable oil

**Method:**
1. In a wide skillet or a big pan, heat the oil over medium-low heat.
2. Stir in the garlic and onion for thirty seconds.
3. Stir in the prawns and the white part of the spring onion for two minutes.
4. Push all aside and pour the eggs on the opposite side. It should only take about 20 seconds to scramble it.
5. Toss in the rice and your favorite sauce.
6. Stir fry for two minutes, halfway through incorporating the green portion of the bell peppers.
7. Mix thoroughly with fresh coriander on top and tomatoes and cucumbers on the bottom.

## 4.14 Vegetarian Pad Thai with Zoodles

**Cooking Time:** 25 minutes
**Serving Size:** 2

**Ingredients:**

**For The Sauce**
- 1 tablespoon honey
- 1-3 teaspoons chili garlic sauce
- 1½ tablespoons rice vinegar
- 1 tablespoon soy sauce
- 2 tablespoons fish sauce

**For the Vegetarian Pad Thai**
- ¼ cup fresh cilantro
- Lime wedges for serving
- 2 large green onions
- ¼ cup peanuts
- 1 cup carrots
- ½ cup shelled edamame
- 2 large eggs

- 1 cup bean sprouts
- 2 medium zucchini
- 2 cloves garlic
- 1 teaspoon olive oil

**Method:**
1. In a shallow saucepan, stir together all the sauce components.
2. Slice the zucchini into zoodles using a spiralizer.
3. In a large skillet over medium heat or broiler, heat one teaspoon of butter over medium-low heat.
4. After the garlic has been added, smash the eggs into the pan.
5. Break the yolk apart like a spoon and simmer for thirty seconds or until it just starts to settle.
6. Stir in the pasta and sauce to combine.
7. Add the green beans, broccoli, edamame, and sliced spring onions and bake till the bean sprouts are crisp-tender, about five minutes.
8. Toss in the coriander and nuts.

## 4.15 Thai Stir-Fry with Coconut Rice

**Cooking Time:** 25 minutes
**Serving Size:** 4
   **Ingredients:**
**Coconut Rice**
- 1 teaspoon sugar
- 1 pinch salt
- 1 can Thai Coconut Milk
- 1 ¼ cups water
- 1 ½ cups jasmine rice

**Thai Vegetables Stir-Fry**
- 1 medium red bell pepper
- 1 small onion
- 2 tablespoons vegetable oil
- 2 cups snow peas
- 1 pound vegetables
- ½ teaspoon garlic powder
- ¼ teaspoon red pepper
- 3 tablespoons flour
- ¼ cup soy sauce
- 1 teaspoon ground ginger
- ¼ cup honey
- 1 cup vegetable stock

**Method:**
1. Wash jasmine rice with liquid.
2. Bring canola oil, liquid, salt, and sugar to simmer in a small saucepan on a moderate flame.
3. Return to a boil with the rice.
4. In a medium mixing bowl, coat the veggies in flour.
5. In a separate bowl, mix the residual flour, stocks, sugar, sesame oil, garlic, garlic powder, and red pepper; whisk until soft.

6. In a wok or broad skillet over medium-high heat, heat one tablespoon of the oil. Toss in some fruits.
7. In a skillet, heat the remaining one tablespoon of oil.
8. Offer with Coconut Rice on the side.

## 4.16 Thai Green Curry with Homemade Curry Paste

**Cooking Time:** 30 minutes
**Serving Size:** 6
  **Ingredients:**
- 2 teaspoon Thai fish sauce
- 3 tablespoon olive oil
- 1 teaspoon ground cumin
- 1 teaspoon black peppercorns
- 8 kaffir lime leaves
- 1 tablespoon coriander seeds
- 4-6 medium green chilies
- 2 lemongrass stalks
- 1 lime
- 2 shallots
- 2 garlic cloves
- Small bunch coriander
- 5cm fresh ginger

**Method:**
1. Stir fry ingredients. Put all of the food items in a mixing bowl and blitz to a mixture.
2. Use right away or hold in the refrigerator for up to three days in a jar.

## 4.17 Rainbow Vegetarian Pad Thai with Crispy Noodles

**Cooking Time:** 30 minutes
**Serving Size:** 4
  **Ingredients:**
**Noodles**
- 1 carrot
- 1 tablespoon sesame oil

- 1 yellow capsicum
- 1 brown onion
- 1 green zucchini
- 1 red capsicum
- 250g Thai style rice noodles

**Sauce**
- 1 teaspoon fish sauce
- 1 teaspoon sriracha chili sauce
- 1 tablespoon rice vinegar
- 1 tablespoon maple syrup
- 3 tablespoon soy sauce

**Garnish**
- 1 packet fried noodles
- Juice of 1 lime
- 3 green onions

**Method:**
1. Prepare the noodles as directed on the package.
2. To make the sauce, mix all of the components in a mixing bowl.
3. Add the soy sauce and onions to the skillet and stir fry for two minutes, then add the vegetables and capsicums and stir fry for another two minutes.
4. Finally, mix in the zucchini for just one minute.
5. Place the cooked noodles in the skillet and pour the sauce over them.
6. Return the veggies to the skillet. Merge the noodles with the sauce.
7. Remove from heat and garnish with spring onions, lemon juice, and fried noodles.
8. Combine all ingredients and serve right away.

# Conclusion

During the wok heating process, the intense temperature of the pan sears the veggies. Their colors appear even clearer and more vivid as a result of this. As a response, wok-cooked meals are often very attractive. On the other hand, deep-frying causes the food to lose its color or become burnt, making it seem less appetizing. For their masterful use of veggies, meats, and fish with reasonable saturated fat and liquids that are not too rich, wok cooking and Chinese food have been promoted as safe and attractive, provided calories are maintained at an acceptable amount. Wok cooking is a nutritious and fast way to prepare a wide range of dishes. Try the wok recipes in the "vegetarian wok cookbook" with wok recipes from Asian countries and prepare healthy vegetarian meals.

Printed in Great Britain
by Amazon